Praise for *Animal Allies*

"Elizabeth Pagel-Hogan makes STEM come alive with her captivating narratives of women scientists in the field. The detailed slice-of-life biographies, written in accessible language, along with sidebars that include fascinating background info and subtle calls to action, create an indispensable volume for the classroom or homeschool library."
—Teresa Robeson, author of *Queen of Physics*

"The women highlighted in *Animal Allies* are funny, smart, and above all else, tough. Reading was more than an inspiration, it was a reminder that women are out there, all over the world, learning, exploring, and figuring out how animals live—all while creating space for future generations of passionate women to work alongside us."
—Dr. Michelle LaRue, associate professor at University of Canterbury

"This is the book I wish I had as a young girl interested in science! Reading the personal stories about these amazing women in biology and learning about their research and careers will without a doubt inspire the next generation of women scientists. This is a must-have book for anyone interested in animals and science."
—Dr. Corrie Moreau, evolutionary biologist and professor at Cornell University

"A timely and terrific book about women in wildlife research. The portraits are fascinating; the additional resources and activities fabulous. *Animal Allies* will inspire young nature lovers everywhere."
—Deborah Hopkinson, author of *Butterflies Belong Here*

"*Animal Allies* inspires girls to explore a career in STEM through the biographies of trailblazing women in wildlife research. This book opens the windows of opportunities and doors of imagination for young women. Every child should have the opportunity to dream about a career path where they can create, imagine, and make a difference in the world."

—**Dr. Artika R. Tyner, author of** ***Justice Makes a Difference: The Story of Miss Freedom Fighter, Esquire***

"I loved this book! The profiles are readable and personal, capturing the passion these women feel for their work protecting wildlife. The conversational style of writing makes science and scientists feel accessible, while connecting specific living creatures to larger environmental issues like climate change and social justice issues like racism and sexism."

—**Mary Cronk Farrell, award-winning journalist and the author of** ***Fannie Never Flinched*** **and** ***Pure Grit***

"Delighted and honored to be part of this book, thank you for including me amongst this group of inspirational, motivated and successful women."

—**Dr. Helen Pheasey, lecturer at the School of Anthropology and Conservation**

ANIMAL ALLIES

15
AMAZING WOMEN
IN WILDLIFE RESEARCH

ELIZABETH PAGEL-HOGAN

CHICAGO
REVIEW
PRESS

Published by Chicago Review Press Incorporated
814 North Franklin Street
Chicago, Illinois 60610

ISBN 978-1-64160-622-6

Library of Congress Control Number: 2022931378

Cover and interior design: Sadie Teper

Printed in the United States of America
5 4 3 2 1

To Chrissy and Denny, thanks for letting me bring home all those pets.

"The time to protect a species is while it is still common."
Rosalie Barrow Edge

Contents

Introduction

Do you feed birds?

Do you wish you had night vision to see the animals that roam your neighborhood?

Do you not squish spiders?

Would you help a turtle safely cross the road and wonder where it's going? (Probably to the shell station.)

Do you wonder what you can do to protect wildlife?

Then this is the book for you.

This book is about 15 scientists from around the world who love learning about living things. They are curious and dedicated. Sometimes they are clumsy too. They have great days, like when they get a photo of a secretive wild cat! They have hard days, like when they face the effects of pollution and climate change.

But they are determined. And they don't keep their discoveries or difficulties a secret. They want you to come on the journey with them! Learn about the science, wonder why, ask questions, and you can be an animal ally too.

Part I : Birds

Corina Newsome:
Saving the Seaside Sparrow

The sharp grasses growing in the salt marshes off the coast of Georgia make it a dangerous place to work.

"The marsh has drawn blood," says Corina Newsome. "It's drawn blood, sweat, and tears."

Corina Newsome is a birder, a Black woman, an activist, and a scientist. She is a researcher working on her master's degree in biology from Georgia Southern University and has spent weeks in the salt marshes off the Georgia coast.

"It smells like a mix between salt and wet dirt," Corina says. In her knee-high wading boots, tank top, and a visor—no hat could contain her braids—she has braved the challenges of the marsh.

"Walking in mud is like walking up stairs the entire time. The first time I went out I was utterly exhausted within 30 minutes," she says.

The marsh is no easy place to study. Before arriving there, she had to get through strips of grass filled with grasshoppers—it seemed like thousands of them. The shrieks and calls of large wading birds like herons and egrets startled her.

"Their calls are terrifying, like dinosaurs. One time I didn't know a tricolored heron was there. It called, and I thought it was a man chasing me. I screamed and ran," she says.

And then there are the sharks.

"I was taking a rest and had my foot in a tidal river, and a dogfish shark swam over my foot. I was stunned," she says.

The marsh isn't just a dangerous place to study; it can be a dangerous place to live, especially for the Seaside Sparrow.

Corina is researching the Seaside Sparrow. It's a tiny grey and brown bird with a flashy yellow patch on its face. It makes its home in the grasses of the salt marsh. The Seaside Sparrow is found along the East Coast of the United States and down to parts of the Gulf Coast. This bird doesn't—and can't—live anywhere else. The female weaves an open cup nest suspended above the ground in the cordgrass. She lays between two and six white, speckled eggs. When they hatch, both the male and female feed the hatchlings. The young birds leave the nest soon after hatching, around 12 days, if they survive that long.

Sometimes, an unusually high tide causes the eggs and chicks to drown if they are too close to the ground. It's a risk all Seaside Sparrows face. But if the sparrows build their nests higher to keep them from flooding again, there are other threats. Predators, including raccoons, mink, and the local rice rat, all stalk the grasses, hunting for the nests. They are easier to find if they are high off the ground. So the sparrows have to build their nests in a perfect place, not too low, where they'll get flooded, and not so high that predators can see them.

Unfortunately, the perfect nest placement will get harder to find. Climate change is causing sea levels to rise. For example, seas have risen seven inches (18 cm) on the coast of Georgia. Tides are coming in higher in the marsh, causing bird nests to fail, and scientists think this will make it harder for them to balance the threat of flooding and the threat of predators.

The birds are stuck between a rock and a hard place.

During her research, Corina set up video cameras to watch the nests. She had videos of eggs hatching, parents feeding, the wind shaking the grasses that hold the sturdy structures.

She also set up camera traps in the nearby area. Camera traps are motion-triggered. They turn on when something moves by them, like a hungry raccoon or rice rat.

Sometimes the videos were difficult to watch. Corina has observed the struggles of sparrows. She's seen rice rats take chicks. And she's watched new dangers arrive. Rising water levels flood more nests and bring new predators, like fish, to prey on chicks. One loss of a chick caught on video was especially hard for her.

"I cried. My heart was broken," says Corina. "These birds are declining in number. Every nesting success for these birds means so much. I imagined what that chick was feeling, but also thought about the larger population. Because of climate change, nest flooding will keep happening. Chicks are going to drown. Plus, now there are new predators."

Despite her heartbreak, Corina knew this video was important.

"No one would have known it happened without scientists doing this research. I felt honored to offer this perspective. I did the work to get this up-close look to provide important info about protecting them. It gave me purpose."

It's not Corina's job to stop the predators—at least not yet. What she's trying to do is first understand the threat from predators. She's looking at how close the nests are to rivers and roads. Does being close to a river or road make a nest more vulnerable?

"There's not a lot we can do to stop flooding water into the marsh," Corina explains. "But there are ways to manage predation threat. If we know predators are more active here, wildlife managers can restrict their activity."

But is restricting predators too much interference with nature? Predators have young to feed too.

"No," Corina says. "The most common predators in the marsh are not under threat at all. In fact, their populations are higher than natural levels."

Corina explains that in wildlife conservation, species are ranked by threat level. The Seaside Sparrow is closer to going extinct than its predators are. Her research will help wildlife managers make decisions, such as protecting the breeding area for these birds to keep predators from wiping out the next generation. They will protect the breeding area for these birds and will prevent predators from destroying the next generation.

"We give priority to the next species in line facing the threat of being endangered or going extinct."

The Bald Eagle's Best Friend

Lucille Farrier Stickel directed the Patuxent Wildlife Research Center in Maryland from 1972 to 1982. She was the first woman to direct a major federal fish and wild-life laboratory. She is called the "bald eagle's best friend" because her work saved the species from the ravages of the pesticide DDT.

Lucille published her first paper on the effects of pesticide contaminants in 1946. Rachel Carson used a lot of Lucille's research to write her landmark book *Silent Spring*.

Lucille's research showed DDT made the eggshells of birds of prey too thin. Thinner eggshells meant young birds could not develop properly. As a result of DDT use, populations plummeted. In 1963, only 417 nesting pairs of bald eagles lived in the lower 48 states. Lucille's work led to the ban of DDT as a pesticide in the United States in

1972. Lucille died in 2006. By 2007, there were over 10,000 bald eagles in the country, and the species was removed from the endangered species list.

Corina's focus on protecting the vulnerable extends beyond her bird research.

"In the same way wildlife management addresses the most vulnerable animal communities first, that's how we have to look at human communities," says Corina. "The people who live on the coast, the people who face poverty and socioeconomic struggles are the most vulnerable. For too long, the concerns of people with money and power have been at the center of how we make decisions. That's what gotten us to the environment emergency. We need to center people who are vulnerable."

Corina is no stranger to threats.

"People say racist things to me in the workplace," she says. "There's been anti-Black racism in many of my workplaces."

Even in the field, she doesn't feel completely safe.

"Have I felt like my safety is compromised out in the middle of nowhere? In a place full of Trump signs and Blue Lives Matter? Yes, that context feels threatening," Corina says. "But I'm a light-skinned Black woman. My experience is not reflective of Black men and dark-skinned people. There's never been a time when a person called the cops on me directly."

Her family and friends have experienced these threats. Even when aimed at people Corina doesn't know personally, threats to Black people affect her life and her community.

Corina was part of a large social media community of Black people in natural science and STEM (science, technology, engineering, and mathematics) fields. In 2020, a fellow birder, Chris Cooper, was threatened by a woman in Central Park who called the police and falsely claimed he was threatening her life. Corina and others in the group took action. They established a week to recognize Black birders and bring awareness to safety concerns facing Black people enjoying nature. They called it #BlackBirdersWeek.

One person offered to do graphics, another person organized a timeline of events, and the project took off in about two days. Corina worked on communications.

"A lot of my job was reaching out to the public," Corina says. She did an interview with the National Audubon Society. She wanted Black birders to be seen and heard.

#BlackBirdersWeek

Black Birders Week is a weeklong event highlighting Black birders in the United States.

Black Birders Week has three main goals. The first is to remind the public that Black people belong in the outdoors. Young Black people interested in natural science and conservation could be turned away by threats of racism and violence.

The second goal of Black Birders Week is to teach the outdoor-loving community about the threats that Black birders face. White people need to hold each other accountable on countering racism.

The third goal is to encourage more diversity in birding and conservation. More birders means a richer, healthier community.

There are thousands of different kinds of birds in the world. Birds come in all shapes, sizes, and colors. They sing unique songs. And they know how to make themselves heard.

So it makes sense that Corina, a birder, scientist, and activist, is also making herself and other Black birders heard.

Corina is from Philadelphia, Pennsylvania. She grew up loving animals but never thought it was possible for her to pursue a career in the environment.

"I loved animals, but being a veterinarian was all I knew," she says.

Then a friend from her church reached out to her.

"He heard I loved animals," she says. "He told me his sister worked at the Philadelphia Zoo and he would introduce me to her."

Corina's friend was Black, like her and everyone at her church. This kind of connection, between a church friend and professional in the field, is often much too rare for Black scientists.

"I assumed she worked in concessions," Corina says. "Because in my whole life I had never seen a Black wildlife professional."

It turns out the woman, Michelle Jameson, was the lead carnivore keeper at the zoo. Michelle took Corina on a tour of the zoo.

"I'll never forget when I rounded a corner and there was a Canadian lynx," Corina says. "She [Michelle] took me under her wing."

Meeting Michelle changed Corina's trajectory. Corina got an internship at the zoo and an introduction to a career she never knew existed.

After getting her undergraduate degree, Corina worked at the Nashville Zoo. She was the only Black person at the zoo working in animal care.

"I was training and caring for animals and doing animal shows for the public. I was seeing thousands of people a day," Corina recalls. "But there was this one instance in one of the animal shows. A Black family stayed behind and the dad came up to me. He said, 'My daughter cannot believe you are doing this job.' I told him I completely understand. I knew what they were seeing. It was like the first time I saw a Black person doing this work. Even before I shared any of the information about the animals, it was being seen, and saying, 'I see you.'"

Corina has an undergraduate degree in zoo and wildlife biology from Malone University. She has been obsessed with birds since her junior year of college when she met her "spark bird." A spark bird is what people in the birding community call the bird that ignites someone's love of birds and birding.

"My professor was giving a slide show of the 10 most common birds in northeast Ohio. He showed a robin, a cardinal, and then he flashed up a slide of a bird I had never seen before. It was a blue jay. I literally shouted, 'What is that!'"

Corina laughs at the memory of this moment.

"I had heard of a blue jay, but I had always pictured it as what a bluebird looks like. Then after class I went outside and realized they were everywhere. What else are people not noticing?"

Seeing things like a spark bird for the first time can change a person's perspective forever. This is why having scientists who look like all kinds of people is important.

"When I had White educators, I was still eating the information up," Corina says. "But there's something about a Black person sharing information with me, it's a totally different experience."

Corina wants to share this feeling with others. Just like her work at the Nashville Zoo, she spends time mentoring young people in animal and environmental science. She is a role model for those who never saw themselves in science.

"To be the one to usher them into this excitement, whether that happens on bird walks, or when I bring high schools behind the scenes at a zoo, it opens a door," she says. "It's not about me, but it's the honor of being the one to direct them."

Corina's parents didn't have money to send her to zoo camps or other wildlife experiences. She had no connections to the field. She didn't even know what the options were.

"That experience is why I started these programs; I want to be as visible as possible," Corina says. "Young people need to see more than one person and discover there are way more Black people in wildlife science than ever imagined."

Social media has been incredibly useful for Corina's goal of reaching out to and uplifting young people. Corina tweets as @Hood_Naturalist. Her website promotes "Conservation. Education. Exploration." On her blog "From the block, to the zoo, to the marsh," she writes about how birds changed her life. She also writes about the links between caring for the environment and fighting racism. She frequently gets messages from kids asking her how they can start learning about a career in working with wildlife.

"Much of the science community in the United States has been fairly homogenous, demographically speaking, for a long time," says Corina. "I know from experience that the science community thrives when more diverse perspectives are represented in its ranks, especially when it comes to interfacing with our diverse general public."

Corina learned a lot in the marsh. It was full of diversity. There were crabs, sharks, dolphins, and, of course, birds. It was harsh and demanding. But it was also beautiful and enchanting.

The marsh is eroding now—and disappearing. And it's not putting only the Seaside Sparrows at risk.

"As the marsh disappears, there's less to absorb storm surges, and it's going to lead to even more damage," Corina says. "When you don't care about the coastal communities, everyone suffers. These people have suffered. If we invest more in the resilience of our coasts, both people and the environment, you help *everyone*."

"I learned so much in the marsh. But I know I don't want to go again. I want to focus more on the community engagement side of conservation, getting communities that are not represented to be centered," she says.

Corina now has a full-time job with Georgia Audubon as the community engagement manager. She wants to create a healthy world where all kinds of people, and animals, not only survive but also thrive.

Social Media

Instagram: @hood__naturalist (two underscores)

Twitter: @hood_naturalist (one underscore)

Michelle LaRue:
Antarctic Satellite Spy

Dr. Michelle LaRue spies on emperor penguins from space. She uses satellites to take photos of their colonies. In the photos, each emperor penguin is a tiny black fleck, but those flecks tell her a lot.

"The photos can tell us how many there are, if they are huddling together or spread out, and how the colony shifts through a season and between seasons," says Michelle.

Michelle is a wildlife ecologist and an associate professor at the University of Canterbury in New Zealand. She's a White woman from Minnesota in the United States. And in Aotearoa New Zealand context, she is *pākehā*, or a foreigner. She's visited Antarctica over six times between 2008 and 2018, as a field leader and principal investigator.

Who Saw Antarctica First?

For about two centuries, most stories about the first people to visit Antarctica included only European explorers.

But oral histories and research show Māori explorer Hui Te Rangiora and his crew were the first people to visit the southernmost continent sometime in the seventh century.

"Hui Te Rangiora (also known as Ūi Te Rangiora) . . . is said to have 'roamed the Pacific as though it were a lake' . . . and in some narratives Hui Te Rangiora and his crew continued south—a long way south. In so doing, they were likely the first humans to set eyes on Antarctic waters and perhaps the continent," writes Dr. Priscilla Wehi, associate professor at the Centre for Sustainability, University of Otago, New Zealand.

When European explorers finally found their way south, the Māori provided navigation and sailing expertise for those explorations, but their skills and contributions were rarely acknowledged or even mentioned, according to Dr. Wehi and other researchers.

Michelle has a lot of firsts. She was the US lead on the first-ever global census of emperor penguins. She was a colead on the first ever census of Adélie penguins. And she was the principal investigator for the first-ever global census of Weddell seals. All three projects were conducted using satellites in space.

Michelle uses GIS, or a geographic information system, which allows researchers to see and manipulate images from space. With this technology, they can count individual Weddell seals and estimate populations of penguins, which helps them understand population status and trends.

"I'm a very spatial person; I need to see things to understand," she says. "Higher math for me was a struggle. It was hard to 'see.' But maps are 'AH!' If I can see the maps of Antarctica, if I can see the different emperor penguins' colonies and Adélie penguins, it works."

Michelle didn't start out studying penguins.

"I wasn't headed *to* anything—this happened by accident," Michelle says. She did her master's work using GIS analysis with mountain lions. That led to a job doing forest inventory, and that led to a job doing cartography with the US Antarctic program. While making those Antarctica maps, she got access to satellite images.

"I saw seals on the ice in the photos. I said, oh my gosh, this is opening up a whole new understanding of animals in Antarctica," says Michelle. Then researchers from the British Antarctic Survey called and asked for a collaborator to estimate emperor penguin colonies using satellite imagery. Michelle volunteered.

Satellites go overhead every 90 minutes in polar orbits. Michelle's team requests images and hopes for clear days with no cloud cover.

"It takes a few days or even months to get the images," she says. "But when we get the images, the fun begins. The actual image analysis can get old after awhile, but at the end you have population estimates for every single emperor penguin colony."

When she began the research, it was just because it was possible.

"Now we do it because we want to know what they are doing! They are so weird," Michelle says. "For example, Adélie penguins are supposed to nest on land, not ice. But we found Adélie penguins on the ice because of their guano stain. They were in a group and evenly spaced as though they were nesting. We went to that spot in a helicopter and were able to verify and count exactly how many there were—462 Adélie penguins. To my knowledge this was the only time they did this."

Ground validation of these discoveries is very important, which is why Michelle goes to Antarctica instead of only looking at photos in a lab.

"The thing about remote sensing is that it's interpretation, so it's critical to have that check on the ground. I think I'm looking at 'this'—but is that right?" Michelle explains. "We also need to understand what we're looking at in the environment and habitat. But the nice thing about satellites is that you don't have to be everywhere, and you don't have to go all the time."

Satellites also can't capture the smells of being on the ice.

"When you get off the plane it smells cold, and in town it smells like rocks, like metal, and very dry," she says.

And photos don't include the sounds of the Antarctic.

"Whipping wind screeching past your ears," she says. "There's also the popping and creaking of the ice; if you sit long enough, you'll hear it. The last sound is the quiet. You hear nothing. One night we were camping in the McMurdo Dry Valleys, and I have never had such a quiet experience in my entire life. No wind. No snoring. I remember being awake and thinking, 'I have never not heard something.'"

And being on the ice means getting up close and personal with the wildlife.

"The first time I came across elephant seals, holy hell. [The smell] wasn't exactly vomit-inducing, but it was bad," Michelle remembers. "Out at the penguin colonies it smells like fish. It smells awful. You can tell when you're nearby one."

The penguins can also tell when people are nearby.

"Emperor penguins are very curious," Michelle says. "On one visit to Erebus Bay, we saw them way off in the distance. Twenty minutes later they came over, and we had to stop what we were doing and sit there to adhere to environmental protocols. You can't alter their behaviors. If one was 10 feet away and I approached and it moved, that would violate the Antarctic Conservation Act. We had to wait for an hour! It was pretty funny. They were taking a long time to check us out."

Michelle has always been comfortable around animals. Her grandparents had a farm, and on school assignments she listed *zookeeper* or *dolphin trainer* as her ideas for future jobs.

"I have a passion for being around animals," Michelle says. "When I was a kid, I trained dogs in dog agility. We were encouraged to have animals in our lives. Everybody loved animals, and we especially loved to understand them."

In high school, she really enjoyed anatomy and physiology and considered veterinary school. But in college, her career goals changed.

"I remember distinctly a professor had a slide show of the fun stuff he had done as an ecologist," Michelle said. "I followed him back to his office and switched my major to ecology."

In high school, at least half of her science teachers were women. But as she moved into wildlife ecology, it became clear the field was male dominated.

Women Doing Science in Antarctica

In 2016, the Scientific Committee on Antarctic Research (SCAR) hosted a Women of the Antarctic Wikibomb. A Wikibomb means creating a large amount of Wikipedia entries in a short time to promote awareness about an unknown issue or group of people. Dr. Jan Strugnell and Dr. Thomas Schafee led the Wikibomb.

Now people can read about some of the early scientists like Maria Klenova, a Russian geologist. Her first expedition to Antarctica was in 1955.

People can also read about Jeanne Baret, a botanist, who visited the Antarctic region in 1776. Jeanne is considered the first woman to complete a circumnavigation of the globe.

Students studying famous explorers can now research Jackie Ronne, an American who journeyed there in 1947–1948. The Ronne Ice Shelf is named after her.

These stories are just the tip of the iceberg.

"I never had a female advisor," Michelle says. "The first woman I ever worked for was a collaborator who wasn't even my boss. I hadn't realized this until last year, but there was this culture of trying to be women who got along with the guys. Maybe I was ignoring things or didn't recognize what should have bothered me."

Her efforts to get along with people didn't protect her from sexual harassment.

"On the ice, it was pretty rough in some cases," she says. "I must have gotten hit on weekly. Probably the year that was the worst was 2011 or 2012. I felt unsafe. I tried to hide from people. I made sure to never be alone. And this was in addition to not having support from the people I was working for."

Like many people, Michelle had a full-time job while she was getting her PhD.

"The academic side was fantastic," she says. "But some of the people I worked with were really challenging. I faced anything from harassment and intimidation to bullying. My view was 'leave me alone.' I don't think I recognized how wrong it was until after a couple of years."

What Is Sexual Harassment?

According to the United Nations Entity for Gender Equality and the Empowerment of Women, sexual harassment is any unwelcome sexual advance, request for sexual favors, and verbal or physical conduct of a sexual nature. It can be a single offense or an ongoing behavior. It can happen to people of any gender. It can include but is not limited to rape, attempted rape, pressure for sexual favors, teasing, touching, facial expressions, gestures, nicknames, blocking someone's path, following them, and more.

Over the 10 years that she has visited Antarctica, things have improved.

"The first time I was there, I was 25," she says. "Maybe things have genuinely changed, maybe I'm less naive. I'd like to believe they've cracked down on sexual harassment. Even when I was there as a young field leader and didn't know things, all the logistics people I dealt with were fantastic. It was always the other men in town who were jerks. But by 2018, the other people at McMurdo Station, ones I didn't work with directly who could have bothered me, didn't."

The First Women in Antarctica

Who was the first woman in Antarctica?

Caroline Mikkelson traveled to Antarctica in 1935 on her husband's ship *Thorshavn*. Caroline, a Norwegian, helped row the boat to shore with other sailors. She landed on an Antarctic island in 1935 and on the continent in 1937.

But before Caroline was Ingrid Christensen. Ingrid and her friend Mathilde Wegger saw the continent from the deck of Ingrid's husband's ship in 1931.

Even earlier records show that one woman and three men were rescued from Campbell Island where they had been shipwrecked in 1839. This woman, whose name was never recorded, saw the Antarctic continent.

Another Western woman reached the Antarctic region even before Caroline, Ingrid, and the unknown castaway. Louise Séguin, a French woman, sailed with Captain Yves-Joseph de Kerguélen-Trémarec in 1773. Louise may have been disguised as a boy.

But the combination of biases against women and biases against non-Western cultures have probably hidden even earlier arrivals by women to Antarctica.

Oral histories of Oceanic people tell of two epic explorers, Ui-te-rangiora and Te Ara-tanga-nuku. These Māori women, who were expert sailors, may have reached Antarctica in 650 and 1000 CE, respectively.

Michelle realizes there is still a lot of work to do regarding diversity in her field.

"The stuff I've experienced isn't close to as bad as what non-White people face," she says. "I don't think I saw a person of color, or very few."

There are difficult moments working with the animals too. Once her team found a dead female Weddell seal. They knew it had a pup, and they knew the pup was also going to die. They had no way to save it.

"My cheeks were nearly frostbitten from having tears frozen to my face. That was so hard," she said.

She has also witnessed huge snowstorms that threatened penguin chicks. While scientists can't save every animal, Michelle hopes that in the long run, her work will help the penguins.

"I was invited to be on the International Union for Conservation of Nature (IUCN) penguin specialist group, and

I'm hoping my research can have some impact," Michelle says. IUCN represents the "gold standard" for deciding if a species is threatened, vulnerable, or endangered.

"I am hoping that my research can help provide context to conservation and action plans—whether it's a matter of 'hey, this species is looking OK so far' or 'this species needs urgent action right now.' Conservation decisions should be based on the best science available, and I hope that I can be part of providing the kind of science needed in order to benefit the conservation of biodiversity."

Michelle also works hard to share her work with the general public.

"What we learn can't just be within the scientific literature; it has to be communicated out," she says. "I do a lot of public talks and workshops about science communication."

Michelle also uses social media on a regular basis.

"Twitter has been fantastic, especially with my work with Weddell seals," she says. "We asked people to search for seals on the high-resolution imagery. And I've been able to use Twitter to talk about my work. I tweet out what I can, including obligatory penguin pictures."

Michelle is very familiar with using both social media and photography to study animal populations. She created the popular #CougarOrNot. On Fridays, she shares photos of animals that might or might not be cougars, and followers guess if the photos are of a cougar. Cougars had been hunted almost to extinction in the early 1900s, but regulations allowed the population to rebuild. She hopes to teach people about the big cats and reduce fear.

#CougarOrNot fits with Michelle's approach to science in general.

"I look at it like a puzzle, like detective work," she says. "I'm trying to put a story together to explain what's happening. It's messy, it's hitting a brick wall, it's not knowing what's going on and the frustration that comes with it. You're not going to understand everything. But everything you learn is adding to the overall picture."

Even if you only learn a little piece, each little piece can add so much. And according to Michelle, the mindset of a scientist means being curious but also humble.

"Students always think we need to make the next big discovery," she says. "But everything you find is cool. Adding that little piece might blow things up next year, 10 years, 100 years from now."

Social Media

Personal website: www.drmichellelarue.com

Twitter: @drmichellelarue

Natalia Ocampo-Peñuela: Angry Birds

Dr. Natalia Ocampo-Peñuela has a unique collection.

"I actually collect bird scars on my hands," she says. "I have all these scars from the birds that I've handled that bit me really hard. They're angry; you should get angry when you're disturbed. It's how it should be."

Natalia is a birder and researcher from Colombia. She's the project lead for Expediciones BIO: Alas, cantos, y colores, a special program at the Humboldt Institute that is funded by the Ministry of Science in Colombia. *Alas, cantos, y colores* means "wings, colors, and songs." Natalia and other researchers are revisiting the areas in Colombia surveyed by American ornithologist Frank Chapman over 100 years ago.

"We are trying to retrace their steps, to locate the exact places they went, find the ecosystem that looks the most similar, and survey the birds again," she says. It's often hard to find the sites. The land has changed in 110 years.

"Some places have been devastated, some have a lot of forests, some have been fragmented into smaller pieces," she says.

The first part of her research focuses on a census of the birds. Then she and other researchers do a collection expedition using mist nets. The collection serves as another time stamp, another set of data based on the first collections done by Chapman. The 110-year-old specimens are still used for DNA analysis. From the modern birds, Natalia can collect blood and tissue samples in the field.

Even though Natalia is seeking the same birds as Chapman, her project is different in a lot of ways. The old surveys involved White men from the United States coming in, collecting birds, and taking them back to the American Museum of Natural History in New York City. These bird specimens will stay in Colombia in the museum of the National University in Bogota and will be available to all scientists and the public.

"Past expeditions were led and funded by foreign countries. We have really good elite Colombian scientists leading it and a strong team dominated by women," she says. "We see this goodness of having women in the team; everything works like clockwork. It's inspiring for future generations. It used to be all men, but we set this new example and role models."

Each group has ten expeditionaries and five local biologists. Instead of scientists from other countries, Natalia's expeditions include local researchers. They also use local guides.

"We have a very strong social component; we do a lot of dialogue with the local people to learn from them. We value this local knowledge and all they know about their birds," she says. "And we return with a team of social scientists to share what we have learned and build knowledge."

They aren't sharing the knowledge just to be nice.

"We're going to design a bird-watching route on these sites. We're going to offer a tour," she says. "This will become an economic alternative to these communities. This information will be useful for social and economical purposes for the people. If you conserve these birds and bring tourists, you can have a sustainable income and protect the birds."

Natalia uses social media not only to promote her research but also to share information with the general public.

"When we do an expedition, we do a lot of pictures and mention people. We emphasize how this is a Colombian-run project, led by women. We send these additional messages besides just the science. We are supporting locals and showing these women and how amazing they are."

The data from the Expediciones BIO will be open source and available to anyone. Sharing knowledge with the public is an important part of her philosophy.

"I find that very powerful. It's a way to reach nonscientific communities. We try to communicate in very simple words things that are very complex. We are also trying to reach government and decision makers."

Natalia's work has three main goals.

"I am a spatial conservation ecologist and look at how land changes affect birds. We always want to see areas that are natural and pristine to remain that way. We need it, not everywhere, but in some places. Because those are the sources of population for everywhere else. The second strategy is to conserve while you produce sustainably. You can use the land, we need to, but you can also have little conservation actions that can help a lot. Like if you have crops, you can leave corridors or patches of forest."

Her third goal is to restore landscapes that have been degraded.

"If we restore them to their natural ecosystem, we know that species can come back," she says.

Expediciones BIO started in January 2020. The goal was to match the same dates of the original Chapman surveys. But because of the COVID-19 pandemic, Colombia was on lockdown and Natalia and her team couldn't get out into the field. They spent the lockdown preparing. The country reopened on September 1, 2020, and on September 2 they were in the field.

"We have done two expeditions, one to the High Andes and one to the dry forest," she said. "The dry forest has an acidic plant smell. It had been raining a lot, which was unusual, and all the plants were green. When you walk there you feel this limey smell in the forest. The other smell is dirt on your boots."

Birding fieldwork involves waking up early.

"We leave the camp before sunrise," Natalia says. "As we are walking to the mist nets, it starts very silent. Then there is a peak in the dawn chorus and 30 to 40 species sing at one time. The dawn chorus is when we open the mist nets to try to catch the first activity of the day."

Mist nets are fine mesh nets suspended on poles about nine feet (3 m) high. Birds can't see the nets and fly into them, becoming trapped. Researchers monitor the nets for 12 hours per day, periodically removing birds from the net, processing the birds, and then releasing them. They set 40 to 50 nets in the same portion of land for three days, then move on to a new spot.

"I like the birds that get really angry when you catch them. I think that's what it should be," she says. "It's like a kidnapping. You're caught, put in a bag, transported places. We try to make it the least disturbing as possible."

That's why Natalia has so many scars on her hands. But it's not just birds caught in the nets that get angry. Birds who didn't get caught are angry too.

"The other birds *not* in the net can perceive it. You catch a male or female, and their partner will be calling next to the net," she says. "Or you catch birds that are part of a flock and the rest of the flock will be around you, being very noisy. It inspires us to be careful and do it in an ethical way."

Bites from birds aren't the only challenges that Natalia faces on these expeditions.

"I'm a scientist, but now I'm also a manager, and with COVID, it's been an even bigger challenge. I've discovered skills I didn't know I had," she says. "I'm leading a good team of people who are eager to learn."

Natalia's also faced physical challenges. She was pregnant on both expeditions.

"I had a team that was supportive, and I could support the expedition in ways that didn't mean going down the slope every half hour," she says. "This was one of the reasons I really wanted to go. You can have a team of diverse women. Some are young, some not so young. Some are mothers. It's important that you show people it's not a barrier."

The researchers also tapped into some historic inspiration. On the second expedition, the research group divided to form an all-female group.

"We went to a place where there was a female bird collector, Elizabeth Kerr. She went there and went to collect birds to sell to museum. We did a short expedition honoring her legacy. It was five women in the sub-Andean forest, trying to find places where she had been."

Who Was Elizabeth Kerr?

In 1917, ornithologist Frank Chapman wrote a 600-page book about his visits to Colombia. Buried on page 69 of the book is a reference to "The Mrs. Kerr Collections." Mrs. Kerr is credited with collecting 194 bird skins from the Central Andes at a 3,000-foot altitude. She also collected 200 more skins from the Atrato Valley. This brief mention of a female ornithologist collecting on her own was intriguing. Who was Mrs. Kerr?

Natalia hoped to survey some of the places Mrs. Kerr collected birds. But the full story of Mrs. Kerr's work and life, like those of so many women, is hidden and possibly lost.

The only information Natalia found was an article Elizabeth Kerr wrote about her journeys, published in the July 13, 1912, issue of *Collier's* magazine.

Elizabeth describes how "a great grief . . . caused me to shoulder a gun and march into the wilderness." The cause of her grief is unknown, but we know she loved the jungle.

"There is joy in the wild freedom of it," she said. "My only sorrow is that I have to sell the beautiful and interesting things I get."

Natalia also faces emotional challenges. Euthanizing birds, or killing them humanely, is too hard for her.

"We sacrifice these birds, and we take them to the museum. I've never been able to sacrifice these birds; it's really sad for me," she says. "I know it's important, but it's very emotionally loaded. I've never been able to take the life of the bird. People think scientists do this and don't feel anything. But it's emotionally hard."

Invisible Killer

A 2014 study revealed that about 1 billion birds die each year in collisions with windows, just in the United States.

Birds can't see clear glass. Glass windows also reflect sky or leaves and branches and look like safe and inviting places to fly. At night, inside lights shine through windows. For reasons scientists don't fully understand, these lights attract migrating birds.

Window collisions sometimes kill birds. Other times, the bird is stunned and flies away only to die later or be eaten by outdoor cats.

There are ways to protect birds from these invisible dangers. Go outside and look at your windows. Can you see reflections of trees and leaves? If you can, birds can.

Mark your windows with soap or tempera paint. Another option is decals or stickers. There are also bird tapes, ropes, screens, and nets.

At Duke University in 2016, Natalia led a project to locate the windows that caused the most bird deaths on campus. Thanks to student support and media attention, Duke University took action to cover the windows in bird-deterring dot patterns.

Natalia has studied birds for 15 years. She loves colorful, beautiful birds. Her favorite birds are cotingas.

"The male is super beautiful, some with turquoise and fuchsia. I love the colors. But they are hard to see because they live at the top of canopy. Not much is known about them," she says.

She also loves colorful birds that get angry, like toucans.

"It is so unlikely you will catch them; I have only ever caught four or five," she says, "But you have to wear gloves. They get *so* angry, they will bite off a finger."

She discovered a love for birds during her undergraduate studies at Pontificia Universidad Javeriana in Bogota, Colombia.

"My mom signed me up for a bird-watching course at Rio Blanco Nature Reserve, and I thought, *this is terrible, you have to wake up early*. Mom said she already paid for it, just go. We were mist nesting. We caught a hummingbird."

That hummingbird was a Tourmaline sunangel. They are about 10 cm (4 inches) long. Males have a bright purple spot on their necks. Their bodies are emerald-green, and they have dark wings.

"I thought, *Oh my god, this is what I'm going to do*. I go back to Rio Blanco Nature Reserve every time I can. It is a special place for me," she says.

Natalia's dad is a professor, and her mom runs a nongovernmental conservation organization. Her mom is an important role model for her. But other than her mother, she hasn't found positive female mentors in her profession.

Natalia was also warned not to start a family during her research.

"When I was applying for [my] PhD, I had an interview with an advisor who asked, 'Are you planning to have children? I can't deal with people having children,'" she says. "It was an issue during my postdoc; I had to fight with the advisor to get maternity leave."

Fortunately, her current institution is supportive of her role as a parent.

"Being raised being told you can do anything is helpful. It's important to raise girls from very small with this mindset," she says. "But it's important to teach this to boys too. My partner is very supportive of my career. We've made moves because of my career. It's a sacrifice. To have a successful woman, it takes a supportive partner. You need this balance."

Expediciones BIO is just one of Natalia's many projects. No matter where she works, she will use her knowledge and voice to work for a healthy world.

"The one thing I think is an important component of the type of science I do is to understand how the world works so we can manage it better," she says. "On these expeditions we try to understand what has happened to the birds so we can plan better to prevent extinctions. We try to turn this knowledge into useful actions, not just for the animals [and] the ecosystems, but also the people."

Social Media

Website: www.nocampopenuela.com

Twitter: @birdmapper

Part II: Arthropods

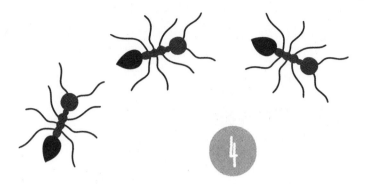

4

Corrie Moreau: Can't Get Enough of Ants

Dr. Corrie Moreau smelled the army ants before she saw them.

"It was like rotting flowers. Slightly sweet, but also a bit like poop. I thought, *What is that?* Then I heard their tiny crinkling, rustling sound," she remembers.

It was an army ant raid. Corrie was in the Amazon collecting other kinds of ants when the column came through. Army ant raid columns can be as large as 24 feet (8 m) across.

"Other insects were flying out of the way. Birds were swooping and diving, catching the insects. There were millions of ants."

Army ants build a bivouac, not a nest. A bivouac is a ball of living ants. In the middle of the ball, protected from predators, are the queen and larvae. The living ants that form the ball can modulate the temperature and humidity. They pull in tight to make it warmer or spread out to cool down.

Army ants build massive colonies and operate on a predictable three-week cycle. They stay in one place for three weeks while the larvae mature. The foragers go out every day to collect food. For another three weeks, they forage while on the move. Then they stop again while new larvae mature.

"Army ants are top predators. Killing a queen is the same as killing a puma in the ecosystem," says Corrie.

Top predators, like pumas and army ant queens, have incredible impacts on their environment. Their kills create food for decomposers, who then enrich the soil and create good growing conditions for local plants. These plants provide shelter and food for smaller mammals, reptiles, birds, and more. The smaller animals become food for larger animals but also eat insects and disperse seeds.

Seeing the army ant raid was unforgettable for Corrie, who has loved ants since she was a little girl growing up in New Orleans, Louisiana.

Growing up in the city meant there wasn't a lot of wildlife for Corrie to observe. There wasn't even a natural history museum. But she did watch every nature show she could find on PBS. And there were always ants around to observe.

"Ants were always my favorite because if you saw one, you would definitely see another," she says. She would scatter crumbs and watch them. She recorded their behavior in her notebook.

Her parents didn't go to college and couldn't guide her career choices. For a long time, Corrie thought she would be either a biology teacher or a pest exterminator.

"At least I'd get to play with bugs then," she laughs. Luckily for bugs and for Corrie, she became a scientist.

"I have the dream job now," she says.

Corrie is a myrmecologist, an ant scientist. She does both museum and fieldwork. She collects samples of insects from different field sites. She brings them back to Cornell University in Ithaca, New York. She is the Martha N. and John C. Moser Professor of Arthropod Biosystematics and Biodiversity and the director and curator of the Cornell University Insect Collection.

"I go to the jungle, collect samples, and bring them to my institution. One representative from each species is on a pin. I put it in the museum collection. It's my voucher for my work," she says.

Her work is building a family tree for ants.

"We grind up an individual ant and use their DNA to infer the evolutionary family tree for ants. We can determine which ants are relatives and examine trait evolution. For example, we may want to know how spines on ant armor evolved. Did spines on the ants' armor evolve once and all the ants with spines are each other's closest relative? Or did spines evolve independently many times across the evolutionary history of ants?"

Corrie also looks for information about ants living around the world.

"How did ants spread across the globe? Where did they first appear? In places like South America or Africa, ants are as old as when continents were one big continent," she says.

The Rarest Ants

Dinosaur ants, or dawn ants, are a rare and endangered species found only in South Australia. They are considered to be living fossils.

Like all ants, dinosaur ants live in colonies. They all leave the colony at dusk, and all return at dawn. Their hunting grounds are eucalyptus trees. They hunt for nectar or prey insects.

Unlike other ants, dinosaur ants don't work together as they hunt. Dinosaur ants don't have different jobs, unlike most other ant species. And they are completely nocturnal.

Climate change means these unique creatures could truly disappear.

Dinosaur ants will not leave their nests if the temperature is warmer than 5 degrees Celsius. As climate change brings warmer global temperatures, ants may not leave the colony at all to forage for food. They could starve and die.

Researchers also fear that bush fires could eliminate the trees these ants rely on and wipe out the species.

After high school, Corrie moved to California. She needed to live there for a year to qualify for in-state tuition at San Francisco State University. She also took out lots of student loans and worked full time while in school.

Corrie worked hard her first year of school. A teacher's assistant noticed her interest in insects and introduced her to Dr. Greg Spicer, who taught arthropod biology. His course was not for freshmen, but he allowed Corrie to enroll. She excelled. Dr. Spicer asked Corrie to work in his lab extracting DNA from insects.

But no one at the university was specifically working on ants. Then the curator of the California Academy of Science, Brian Fisher, came to campus. He met Corrie and offered her a chance to work with him studying ants in Madagascar. She accepted and studied there for three months.

There, Corrie met some ants with unusual feeding habits, called Dracula ants.

"Adult ants feed larvae, but the larvae also feed adults. Ants have narrow waists, which means they can only drink liquid. They can't eat solid foods. But ant larvae can eat anything. So ants feed their larvae other insects. Then adults drum on larvae, and the larvae regurgitate some liquid. That helps the ants get the protein they need."

But Dracula ant larvae won't regurgitate.

"Adult Dracula ants bite a hole in their own larvae and drink their hemolymph, the ant version of blood," Corrie explains. "It doesn't harm the larvae."

Corrie loved studying these ants so much she got a tattoo of a Dracula ant, among several other ant tattoos.

Corrie also spent a month in South Africa learning about curating and museum science. She moved quickly on the path to get her master's degree, and then her doctorate. Throughout her studies, her mentors were helpful, but they were all men.

"As an undergrad I didn't think about it too much, but it was very apparent that there were not a lot of women faculty. I was fortunate there were women grad students and postdocs, but it was clear to me there were not a lot of women in the sciences," says Corrie. "So when I was looking for a PhD, I did want a woman mentor. I had two co-supervisors for my PhD, Naomi Pierce and E. O. Wilson. I wanted to see a woman successful in a role I wanted to be in."

Her PhD project took her to Ecuador and Peru for four months.

"I got to the Amazon and thought *this is how it's supposed to be*. There were bugs everywhere and so much cool wildlife. I grew up in the South. I was used to being hot and sweaty. I was digging for ants, watching tamarins go running across the trees overhead, hearing the screaming piha bird."

Corrie stayed at field stations and sampled ants from different habitats, from different sides of the Andes, and near different rivers. She met the army ants on this project, but she also met more scientists.

"There were all kinds of scientists doing projects. Someone studying tanagers, another studying tapirs. The bird people were up at 4:00 AM. The bat people were up all night. Insect people had a normal schedule," Corrie says.

Corrie noticed there was a greater diversity of scientists in field stations.

"We have equal numbers of women as men starting out but lose women with each move to a new academic rank," she says.

Corrie has visited the Amazon about 10 times. She's had memorable moments there.

"One of my goals was to see a sloth. One day we're walking through the forest and I saw a baby sloth that had died. It sucked all the wind out of me," she remembers.

But she's had funny moments, too. She'll never forget collecting turtle ants in French Guiana in 2017.

"Turtle ants nest inside of hollow twigs in the canopy. They are usually deprived of nitrogen, so they lick bird droppings or mammal urine. We bait them down by tying urine cups to a tree."

(Where did she get the urine? Friendly scientists at the field station volunteered to share theirs!)

"The ants fall in and we collect them. One day, I was gathering them all and pouring all of the collected ants and urine into one container," Corrie says.

(Any idea how this story ends?)

"The urine in one of the cups was putrefied. It was disgusting," Corrie remembers. "I was standing someplace unstable, and it spilled all down me! I had to walk a mile back to the field station covered in putrefied urine."

(Gross.)

How to Collect Ants

Scientists collect ants in many ways.

"We use pitfall traps. We dig a little hole and put a plastic container in the hole so it's level with the soil. Wire holds up the lid like an umbrella. Insects fall in and can't get out," Corrie says.

Bush beating means hitting leaves and foliage and catching whatever insects fall down into an upside-down umbrella.

Another method is leaf litter sampling.

"We pick a meter-by-meter area and chop up leaves and

sticks with a machete. Then we put all that chopped-up material into a sifter and shake it. The sifted material falls into a bag. Back at the lab, as the material dries, the arthropods dive down looking for moisture and fall out on to a collection container filled with preservative."

Another collection tool is an aspirator. An ant biologist holds a glass tube with a piece of fine mesh at the end. The biologist sucks an ant into the tube—slurp.

But the ant doesn't go in the scientist's mouth. It gets stopped by the mesh. Then the scientist blows the ant out—puff—into a collection tube for later study.

As she studies ants, Corrie is also busy creating opportunities for the next generation of scientists. She created the Field Museum Women in Science program when she was at the Field Museum of Natural History in Chicago in 2013.

"The science community is mostly dominated by White men, and I know it's because people haven't been given opportunities," she says. "So I wanted to highlight the work of people with disabilities, people of color, and women. The general public needs to see role models that don't look like what's in textbooks."

The Field Museum Women in Science program runs a monthly seminar featuring a woman who shares her research.

There is also a paid internship for 10 high school students and 10 undergraduate students.

"We know that if we expose women early to the power of research, it's more likely they will stay involved," says Corrie. "But having the paid internship was very important. I wanted to make sure that women who had to have a job had the opportunity to learn."

Maria Sibylla Merian

Generations of children who learned the butterfly life cycle in school can thank Maria Sibylla Merian. She was a pioneer in studying entomology and ecology. She especially loved studying and painting caterpillars and butterflies.

Maria was born in Frankfurt, Germany, in 1647. In the 1600s, people didn't know where insects came from, how they grew, or how they made more insects. Some people thought sunshine turned drops of dew into insect eggs. Others thought fire turned into wasps with painful stings!

Maria noticed things other people overlooked. She collected caterpillars called silkworms and put them in jars. She fed them mulberry leaves. She observed the caterpillars as they formed cocoons. She was there when the moths emerged.

Keeping insects in boxes and jars was not something good German girls did in the 1600s. The wrong word from someone could mean she was accused of witchcraft.

But Maria took the risk.

Maria's studies were one of the first to prove spontaneous generation was wrong. She confirmed that insects (and even toads) are born from eggs.

Corrie, who is White, is an advocate for diversifying science. For her, social media is an amazing platform to share science and find collaborators. It's a way to amplify voices of people who don't have a platform.

"I grew up in low-income housing well below the poverty line," Corrie says. "At first I tried to hide all of that. I was embarrassed. I am also heavily tattooed with images of insects, and it's very unusual for women to be tattooed. I spent time hiding parts of me, but at some point it flipped. I didn't know other students who grew up in poverty, or faculty with tattoos. Then I decided to show it off."

Corrie's experience with poverty informs her work with students today.

"You can't predict who's going to be successful in science. Because I am often involved in making decisions about graduate students, I think about what are traits that make someone successful in science. It's not intellect, it's not knowledge. It's that you as a person have to be curious, creative, dedicated, resilient."

But even with those traits, she knows first hand that the scientific community isn't always welcoming.

"In 2006, I was in graduate school, [and] I had come up [with] an idea to use molecular tools to infer the family tree of ants and couple the information with fossils in order to put dates to it. It was really ambitious. I got an internal Harvard grant. Then we find out that a team of ant biologists, who were all White males, got a giant National Science Foundation grant to do the same thing."

Because they'd be working on similar goals, Corrie reached out to the other team.

"I wrote them an e-mail and explained how our projects were similar and offered to collaborate," she explains. "The head of that team came to Harvard. We discussed how we could collaborate and how I'd get what I needed for my dissertation. He agreed to collaborate during the visit and then went back to the team, and I didn't hear from him. I kept sending e-mails. He finally e-mailed and said, 'no, you should do other work.'"

Corrie felt shocked, disappointed, and overlooked. She offered to return the money, but luckily, the Harvard foundation team asked if she thought she could do it. She said she could. And she did.

"I worked harder than I ever had, six to seven days a week, 10 to 12 hours. Within one year, I had the data and sent my research to *Science*."

Her work showed that ants were at least 40 million years older than scientists estimated and that flowering plants played an important role in their burst in species through time. She let the other research team know about her results. They were not happy that Corrie was first to publish.

"I was a grad student, and they were faculty leaders who told me I have no place here. It lit a fire in me," Corrie says.

The male researchers published later in the same year and showed everything she had published was correct.

Corrie's favorite part about science might be when answering one question opens up more questions.

"We don't know what most ants eat, or where they keep their nests. There's still so much biodiversity out there. There are 15,000 species of ants that have scientific names. But there are double or triple the species waiting to be discovered."

So, there are more questions than ants-ers.

These unanswered questions are just waiting for curious, dedicated scientists to ask.

Social Media

Website: www.moreaulab.org

Twitter: @CorrieMoreau

5

The Bug Chicks: Insect Icons

"Put up a picture on social media of a bug, and the first thing that comes back is a 'kill it with fire' meme," says Kristie Reddick, one of The Bug Chicks. "That's why we start our *Incredible Arthropod* workshops by talking about fears. I ask, 'Do you want to know how I got from being scared to chasing camel spiders?'"

The Bug Chicks are Kristie Reddick and Jessica Honaker. They are entomologists, business owners, and educators. In addition to their research in Africa and the Amazon, they developed a social emotional curriculum for grades 6–12 using insects to talk about tough issues.

They want to help people change how they see bugs, themselves, and the world.

"We use bugs to talk about biases against animals, colors, feelings, assumptions," explains Kristie. "It's a way for students to challenge perceptions of the world, and themselves. We have this lesson called Blending In. We teach about leaf insects and walking sticks. They have behavioral camouflage. You blow on them and they move like leaves and twigs. Then we ask, 'Have you ever blended into a group so much you feel like you disappeared?' Voicelessness in girls is huge. Somewhere around the age of nine, those girls who were first to raise their hands, a lot of them start to shrink. It's not always about being shy in front of boys, it's also about fear of judgment from other girls."

When they teach their workshops, Kristie and Jess try to listen to every student's story of encountering a bug. There are lots of stories, and they often stay late.

"We say, 'That must have been scary.' We are validating their experience," Kristie says. "Then we say, 'Have you ever had a bad experience with a person? Do you not deal with people anymore?' That's when the Tetris piece clunks in. They say, 'Oh, I see what you're doing.' We ask them, 'What if for the next hour we change *eww* to *cool*? Just for the next hour. We promise—you will feel different.' People like to be challenged when they feel like they have ownership in the challenge."

The Bug Chicks have traveled all over the world for research. But they especially love their annual adventure with teens aged 13–17 in the Peruvian rain forest. The week is hosted by JASON Learning, a nonprofit science curriculum company, and according to Kristie, "It's the greatest week of our lives."

For many students, it's their first plane trip. It takes three airplanes and a three-and-a-half-hour boat ride to get to their research location in the Amazon.

"We love the smell of the Amazon," says Jess. "You smell the river water and the rich clay. It's musty, like clothes that never quite dry, but in the best way. You smell plants. You smell the wet earth and your own sweat. It settles over you like a blanket. And sometimes you smell animals, but that is fleeting."

They focus on teaching the students how to do research, a crucial skill.

"We live in a world where people think research is Googling," Kristie says.

Students design their own research questions, like *What is the vacancy rate of tarantula burrows between trails to lodges?*

"They learn there's no right or wrong. And when you get an answer you're not expecting, they learn that no data *is* data," says Jess.

Jess and Kristie bring their students to the local Llachapa community high school. The local students don't speak much English; they speak Spanish and the local dialect.

"Our students learn how to communicate, and their students teach our students—it's beautiful," says Jess. "The kids don't speak each other's languages, but there are zero problems communicating. It's hope for the future and the world."

Threats to the Amazon

Jess and Kristie are passionate about protecting the Amazon Rainforest and the Maijuna, a community of about 500 people who recently reclaimed their ancestral lands after a long battle with the government. Through workshops facilitated by One Planet, a US-based nongovernmental organization that works to facilitate conservation-centered projects with indigenous communities, Kristie and Jess learned about native stingless bees and traditional methods of honey production used by the Maijuna.

Now, a proposed road threatens the Maijuna lands and their livelihoods. City expansion that provides opportunity for one group of people can destroy delicate natural habitats and the people who rely on them. To learn more and see how you can help, visit https://www.oneplanet-ngo.org.

"We speak the language of bug," Kristie says. "Everybody has had an encounter with an arthropod. It's a common language that provides a way to have an experience with other people that is profound."

Not every student on these research trips starts out loving bugs.

"In five days, we have them holding tarantulas and doing research on orchid bees," explains Kristie. "We had a student so terrified of bugs that her mother told her to sleep with bandanas over her ears and mouth because bugs will crawl in. On day one, she was freaking out over a beetle that plays dead. But at the end of day one, she had taken both bandanas off," Kristie says. "On day three, she held a giant tractor tread millipede. On day five, she held a giant pink-toed tarantula. You have to have patience and respect for people's opinions and fears. And there has to be trust."

Safe Bug Collecting

You don't need special clothes or a lot of special equipment to be a bug scientist. You need a container or a jar and curiosity.

Steer clear of animals that can sting, like bees or wasps or biting creatures.

Use a plastic food container (like an empty yogurt container).

To look at the bugs after you've caught them, open your container at an angle. Bugs fly *up*. If you look down into the open container, the bug will fly into your face.

Remember that insects can be really fragile. If you aren't careful, you can hurt them accidentally.

Observe bugs by sitting still near flowers. Then visit a different habitat and document what's different about the bugs you see. Digital collections (taking pictures and videos) are a great way to collect bugs.

Keep bugs in containers out of direct sunlight. After you've observed a bug and taken photos, release it. Don't keep bugs longer than 10 minutes.

"Kristie and I are really good at speaking the language of kid in terms of empathy," says Jess. "A lot of adults discount kids' thoughts and opinions and say 'they're just kids.' When you treat a young person with empathy and respect, and provide positive peer pressure and support, that's one of the things that allows us to connect with kids on a level where other teachers and educators may not."

Kristie has firsthand knowledge of the power of an educator.

"I grew up wanting to study animals in Africa or blue whales, the bigger the better," says Kristie. "In eighth grade I had to test into a marine biology course and a teacher told me I had no aptitude for science. She said I should stick to stage and dance. I went, *Oh, OK, she's a teacher, she must know.*"

Kristie was a dedicated dancer, putting in 40 hours a week. She went to college for theater, but after breaking her shoulder in a horseback riding accident, reconsidered what she wanted. She went back to school to study evolutionary biology. Thanks to an enthusiastic professor, she fell in love with bugs.

Jess, who is White, also didn't start out loving bugs. She studied physical therapy as an undergraduate at Marshall

University. A class in invertebrate zoology converted her to arthropods.

Her favorite bug?

"I have a rotating favorite, but aphids are always near and dear to my heart," said Jess.

In 2005, Jess and Kristie met in graduate school at Texas A&M University, in College Station, Texas, in an insect photography course. Surrounded by like-minded peers, encouraging professors, and supportive staff, they were both able to fully lean into their love of arthropods. But the road to becoming a woman in science wasn't without obstacles.

Once, a male classmate came to Jess's apartment to study but ended up making unwelcome physical advances on her. She threw him out of the apartment. She never shared this experience with her fellow students because she wasn't sure she would have their support.

"It derailed a few classes for me," Jess said. "I had to see this person. It was a small group, and everyone knew everyone. And I thought, *If you kick up a big stink, what's going to happen?* In hindsight, I wish I'd said something. I don't blame myself, but I would address it differently now. Speaking up is hard. It takes practice."

Kristie faced her own challenges. She started an educational video production company called Solpugid Productions in 2005. For graduate school, she wanted to go to Kenya to study camel spiders and needed someone to film her as she did her research and taught in schools. Science education was an integral part of Kristie's thesis, and she knew that was where her career was headed.

Kristie had discovered her love of camel spiders, also known as solifuges, during a previous trip to Kenya in 2003 when she studied large mammals. One night, she heard a scream from a friend, grabbed her bug net, and encountered her first camel spider.

"It was big and the color of dried blood. It looked like it had 10 legs. The front two legs are actually mouthparts. They have suction cups and can climb up walls. It opened its jaws and hissed-screamed at me. If love at first sight exists, that was it. It's quite small compared to mammals, but it had an attitude that would not quit. It had presence and charisma."

During their first semester in grad school, Kristie asked Jess to go with her to Kenya. Jess put her own research on hold to travel with Kristie.

"Our professors didn't like it," Kristie remembers. "Who is this blond girl messing with the system?"

Neither one minded messing with the system. Kristie already felt she had a reputation as an outlier in the department.

"I didn't come from a traditional science background, but I believe in asking for what you want," says Kristie.

Kristie was awarded a fellowship from the LT Jordan Institute for International Awareness. It wasn't a lot of money, but it would get her to Kenya to pilot her research. If she could find camel spiders, her professor said they could find more money to do a full research project.

Kristie needed special permission to travel for her research. So she worked hard to get the required signatures from every level of administration up to the university vice provost. At a banquet, she had a chance to thank the vice provost for permitting her to travel.

"I said I wouldn't let him down," Kristie says. Then he looked her up and down and said, "If I had known what you looked like, I *never* would have signed that paper." Kristie is a tall, blonde, White woman. She believes the vice provost judged her appearance and didn't think she was capable of doing the fieldwork.

Jess and Kristie remember being shocked by his comment.

"I think all I said was 'too late now,'" Kristie says. She went to Kenya in 2006 by herself. "And I found solifuges."

Sort of a Spider, Sort of a Scorpion

Solifuges have a lot of nicknames. They are called camel spiders, wind scorpions, or sun spiders. They are arachnids, but solifuges aren't true spiders or scorpions.

They can grow to about six inches (15 cm).

Solifuges are best known for their really large, really powerful chelicerae, or mouthparts. These mighty mouthparts are also called jaws or fangs. They can be as big as one-third of a solifuge's body.

Solifuges live in deserts around the world. They hunt at night and eat other arthropods, small lizards, birds, or mammals in their size range.

Solifuges are fast and can run up to 10 miles (16 km) an hour. But they get tired after running a short distance. Solifuges aren't venomous and aren't a threat to people. People often think a solifuge is chasing them when it's really chasing the cool shade of a human's shadow.

While all arachnids have eight legs, solifuges look like they have 10 legs. But those extra appendages are actually pedipalps. Pedipalps are mouthparts. Solifuges use pedipalps for moving, feeding, and fighting.

In 2007, Jess and Kristie returned to Kenya for six more months.

"One of my favorite things in Kenya was to dig through elephant dung to find tiny purple solifuges. They eat termites that break down the dung," says Kristie. "When I think of Kenya, I smell rich, warm, sun-baked stale hay."

Kristie and Jess created the first live arthropod museum exhibit in all of East and Central Africa.

"Our research partners Joseph Mugambi and Charles Warui took us on a walk-through of the Nairobi Snake Park," Kristie says. The park had snakes, tortoises, and crocodiles. "But when we asked if they had an arthropod section, they said, 'No, we've never done that.'"

They named the exhibit *Wadudu Wazimu*, which means "crazy bugs" in Swahili. The staff were so excited they kept the exhibit for a year and created a position for a Kenyan female entomologist.

"We had a solifuge arachnid on exhibit, and they kept it alive for over a year," Kristie says. "It's very difficult to keep them alive in captivity. They have voracious appetites, and you have to feed them all the time. They tend to run themselves to death. They have a very high metabolic rate, and they're very fragile animals."

Kristie and Jess also worked with Rescue Dada, an organization that helps girls leave the streets. The girls painted a mural in the exhibit.

"Those girls were getting school credit, they were hanging out with scientists and talking bugs," says Jess. "Working with them was a highlight of our trip."

Kristie also had a significant research achievement.

"I named and described a new species of solifuge," she says. "A lot of people will say 'I discovered,' but as a White person I was not the first person to see that animal. I never say 'I discovered.' I named and described a species that was new to science. I named it after Joseph Mugambi, because we never would have survived without him. He was an amazing friend and an incredible scientist."

The solifuge is called *Tarabulida mugambii*.

For Jess, seeing the impact of Kristie's teaching in the communities they visited was a game changer. She told Kristie that she loved the science education work and wanted to join forces.

After they returned home, Kristie and Jess started The Bug Chicks in 2008. They worked with Texas A&M University on several media and consulting projects. They were even highlighted in a museum exhibit about their work in Kenya at the Association of Former Students.

"Even though we had a few road bumps, our professors and the Entomology Department have always had our backs, and we would not have this incredible life without the support they gave us throughout our time there," Kristie says.

"That school opened every door for us," Jess says.

They moved from Texas to Portland to continue doing educational workshops and produce bug videos.

Working with arthropods keeps things edgy and exciting. There is one spider that has created some very special moments for The Bug Chicks.

"When Jess and I were teaching outdoors at a summer camp, we had this pink-toed tarantula. When they are babies, they are bright blue and silver dollar–sized," says Kristie. They are arboreal, meaning they live in trees. They jump from branch to branch.

Jess and Kristie were surrounded by 60–70 fifth-graders. Kristie showed off the spider, named Cookie Monster.

"I bring her out, she's been fine, then a gust of wind hits her hairs, which are quite sensitive," Kristie says.

Cookie Monster jumped.

"She launches out, horizontal, and all I can see are 60 fifth-graders opening their mouths in shock and a bright blue tarantula flying through the air," Kristie says. "When people ask about a nightmare scenario when we're teaching with live animals, this is it. She's a nonnative species, there are 120 human feet, and it's chaos."

Kristie yelled, "NOBODY MOVE!"

Nobody moved.

"I grabbed her, she was fine, and I told the kids, 'We got her back in the cage!' And they all cheered!" Kristie remembers.

But Cookie Monster had more surprises waiting.

"We were filming a workshop, and we had 20 kids in a circle, sitting on the floor, and Kristie has got Cookie Monster," Jess remembers. "The spider turns around, and I hear Kristie go 'no, no!' The spider lifts up her abdomen and pees right in this kid's open mouth."

Actually, it wasn't just pee. It was poo too. Spider droppings are a white, chalky liquid and are a mix of both.

"I shouted, 'Do not close your mouth!'" Kristie says. "Luckily, we knew this kid and had been teaching him since he was little."

Most workshops aren't this dramatic. But when people who are fearful of bugs hold insects in their hands, often something clicks inside.

"When you feel a connection with something you didn't expect to, it's a literal rewiring of how you see the world," says Jess. "If you can find empathy with something so very different appearance wise, what else can you find connection with? Every day you will be confronted with something that will make you uncomfortable or is unfamiliar. That doesn't mean that thing is bad. Keep an open mind. Because every day there is something new; if you don't keep an open mind you close yourself off to all kinds of awesome."

"Different isn't bad," Kristie says.

"Different isn't bad," Jess agrees.

Social Media

Website: www.thebugchicks.com

Twitter, Instagram, Facebook: @thebugchicks

Lizzy Lowe: A Hero for Spiders

In the summer of 2019, Dr. Lizzy Lowe witnessed something unforgettable in the backyard of her home in Sydney, Australia.

"Dead spiders were falling from trees. It was horrifying," she says.

Lizzy wasn't horrified by the spiders. She was worried about them. The spiders died because of the excessive heat in Australia that summer. It was 47 degrees Celsius, or over 116 degrees Fahrenheit.

"It was really scary. Me and my colleagues were worried because all the insects died off, and the flying foxes, too, birds and bats, that's how hot it was," Lizzy says. It was especially hot in the city because of the urban heat island effect. There is more concrete and less shade in cities, so cities get hotter than surrounding areas.

Lizzy is an urban ecologist and postdoctoral researcher at Macquarie University in Sydney. She studies spiders living in cities. Growing up, she was a self-described "bug kid."

"I kept snails, slaters (pill bugs), and spent most of childhood saying I would be a zoologist," she says. "I spent a couple of years at a bush town, and it opened my eyes to nature. I have always loved spiders."

Spiders are the main terrestrial invertebrate predator across the world. This means they are the most abundant, and they eat a huge amount of prey. They are found everywhere except Antarctica.

What Is Biodiversity?

Biodiversity is a broad term that includes "the variety of life on Earth at all its levels," from genetic material to the entire ecosystem, according to the American Museum of Natural History in New York City.

Biodiversity has intrinsic value, which means it is important just for its own sake. But it also has utilitarian value, in that biodiversity can be useful to humans. Biodiversity provides fuel, medicine, food, and shelter. Biodiverse ecosystems also provide services. These include pollinating plants, recycling nutrients, cleaning water, minimizing pests, and even regulating the climate.

Biodiversity can offer a sense of balance and well-being to people and communities, but this is much harder to measure.

Over the last century, human populations have had a

negative impact on biodiversity. As human development destroys ecosystems, species die or are killed. This reduces biodiversity.

But humans can also have a positive impact. Creating national parks, protected marine areas, and wildlife refuges can save habitats and biodiversity.

One of the hardest parts of studying spiders is doing a biodiversity study. The study itself is not complex. It's hard because it's deadly for the spiders.

"When we do a biodiversity survey, the only way we can do it is to kill everything we collect," Lizzy says. "Some we have to get under a microscope or dissect to identify. In the long run it's fine, populations come back. There are hundreds of thousands. But it's hard to kill the stuff you love. I've veered away from biodiversity studies for that reason. But without them we don't know what lives there anymore."

Lizzy is hopeful that new technology, including analysis of environmental DNA, will result in a less harmful method of biodiversity studies.

What Is a Biodiversity Study?

A biodiversity study examines two main aspects of an area: the number of different species and the number of organisms of each species. These two factors are called *species richness* and *relative abundance*. The number of species divided by the number of individuals in an area is the *biodiversity index*.

The American Museum of Natural History shares this example: "A 4-by-4-meter [13-by-13-foot] square area in a carrot patch has 300 carrot plants, all the same species. It has a very low biodiversity index of 1/300, or 0.003.

"A 4-by-4-meter square area in the forest has 1 pine tree, 1 fern, 1 conifer tree, 1 moss, and 1 lichen, for a total of 5 different species and 5 individuals. The biodiversity index here is high, 5/5 = 1."

A healthy ecosystem has a good balance of predators, prey, producers, and decomposers. An unhealthy ecosystem is at risk. It could be overrun by an invasive species or suffer from climate change effects.

In addition to learning more about spiders, Lizzy tries to get people who live in houses and apartments to stop using pesticides on spiders.

"People are using pesticides all over the place. In urban areas we can spray all sorts of nasty stuff we buy at our supermarkets," Lizzy says.

The pesticides are having a devastating effect.

"The insect populations are crashing, and not enough people are studying it," Lizzy says.

Insect Armageddon

In 2018, news outlets reported that a "global crash in insect populations has found its way to Australia, with entomologists across the country reporting lower than average numbers of wild insects." *Scientific American* reported large reductions in insect populations, from moths in Great Britain to fungal weevils in Africa.

And in 2020, scientists published a warning to humanity: insect populations are facing an extinction crisis.

What are the causes? Habitat loss. Nonnative species moving in. Air, water, and light pollution. Loss of plants for food and shelter. Climate change. Insecticides. All these problems are brought about by human activity.

What can we do?

First, more scientists need to study insects.

"The International Union for the Conservation of Nature (IUCN) Red List of Threatened Species has evaluated only some 8,400 species of insects out of one million known to exist," according to *Science Alert*.

We need to know what insects are out there and how many there are. With this information, we can learn more about trends. We can identify areas of biggest declines, and then we can identify the causes of the declines.

Ordinary people can help: even the smallest backyard or garden can become an insect-friendly habitat.

She tells people it's good to have a couple of spiders.

"But spiders are a hard sell," Lizzy admits. "They think every bug in Australia is going to kill them. People haven't died from a spider in over 40 years."

Most spiders are clean animals. They don't give off a smell, and they don't make noises. And even though they aren't dangerous, people are still scared of spiders. Lizzy wants to help reduce some of that fear. Learning about spiders is the first step. She recommends slow, gentle exposure to information and images.

"People don't understand spiders, and there is misrepresentation of spiders of in the media," says Lizzy. "People will say someone got a spider bite, when no spider was ever seen. I would encourage you to do your own research to appreciate the beauty of them."

One of the spiders that could win people over is the tiny peacock spider. They only live in Australia. Males have beautiful color patterns and drum out an irresistible beat to attract females. They dance. And these jumping spiders have another adorable feature.

"They have really good vision, and they will chase a laser pointer like a kitten," says Lizzy.

Many spider species have adjusted to live in human cities. Some actually do better in urban areas. These species are called urban exploiters.

"How we change the environment has changed how they behave," she says.

Huntsman spiders are some of the most well-known Australian urban exploiters.

"They wouldn't usually live in houses, but houses are dry and full of bugs," Lizzy says. Huntsmans eliminate another common household pest.

"Huntsmans are good at eating cockroaches. Would you rather have one huntsman or hundreds of cockroaches?" asks Lizzy.

That's a tough choice for some people, because huntsman spiders are as big as an adult human hand.

And they like ceilings.

"You'll often look up and see one. They are really fast," she says. "But they don't have good vision. So if they see a shadow, they might accidentally run at people. They are confused. They are not doing it on purpose."

It might be hard to remember that when a hand-sized spider is sprinting overhead. But Lizzy hopes people will try.

Lizzy studied golden orb spiders, another urban exploiter, for her PhD work from 2012 to 2016. Golden orbs are weaver spiders. They are found all over the world. Their two front legs point inward, a feature unique to weavers. In most places, females grow to about two inches (5 cm) in size. Males grow less than one inch (2.5 cm).

But in Australia, they get a little bigger.

"Females are usually the size of an iPhone, while males are about thumbnail size," Lizzy says. This size difference is called sexual dimorphism. This is when males and females of a species look different from one another. Golden orbs have one of the most extreme versions of this condition in the animal world. (The angler fish is at the top.)

"I collected 160 golden orb weaver spiders," she says. "I remember driving around with 160 containers of spiders, hoping I don't crash. There's a photo of my car boot chockablock full of spiders."

Lizzy released them around Sydney, Australia.

"I'd be in a park next to people picnicking and releasing these giant spiders," she said. She got some strange looks, but many people wanted to learn more about her research. Lizzy loved sharing the details.

Each spider had a name and a sticker with a number on its back. She'd come back every week and check on them. It wasn't hard to find them.

"It's easy to see their huge webs," she says. By huge, she means around five feet (1.5 m) in diameter. "They stay on that web; they don't want to be anywhere else."

Lizzy studied the size and number of spider babies produced. She didn't count the eggs; she weighed the egg sacs. Her data showed that the golden orbs thrived in the city.

"They are getting more food. There's always rubbish, so that attracts more flies," she says.

Golden orb spiders are just one of the 4,000 known species of spider in Australia. Lizzy estimates there are two to three times that number of undiscovered species. And she notes again that spiders don't pose a huge threat to people.

"Only two of those 4,000 species could kill someone," she says.

When Lizzy does her fieldwork, she wears hiking boots, hiking pants, and a cool shirt. She's never without collecting jars.

"People come to me with arachnophobia and say they are scared of touching spiders," Lizzy says. "You don't have to touch them and probably shouldn't. All of my collection is using a cup and collecting them. The vast majority wouldn't bite you, but if there's no reason to touch wildlife, you shouldn't."

Why Do Scientists Kill Insects and Spiders to Study Them?

Killing insects is part of the process of a biodiversity survey. Entomologists call this collecting. To the general public, collecting seems to go against the goal of conservation. But collecting is essential to entomology.

It's hard to identify insects in the field. They are small, and there are many different kinds of species. Field guides lack a lot of information on all the different kinds of insect and spider species. To accurately identify insect species, scientists need to gather the insects and study them carefully.

But other means of surveying arthropod populations are developing.

EnviroDNA is an Australian company that samples water, soil, or scat (a scientific word for poop) and analyzes the DNA in the sample. By analyzing the DNA, the researchers can determine what species are in the area of the sample. This kind of research can give scientists insights into populations without the need to kill insects or spiders.

Lizzy has big dreams to be a hero for spiders.

"My eventual goal is to get pesticides off the market. I would love to change the policy so it's more difficult to get them. I'd focus on more sustainable pest management, so you only use them when you really have to. But the first step is helping people know they aren't the only option."

Lizzy spends a lot of time doing outreach and public relations for spiders. She focuses on talking to kids about the role spiders play in removing pests.

"I talk about how important spiders are and how much I love them. School kids love bugs; it doesn't take much encouraging. After I go to schools, they are out at the playgrounds looking for bugs. And they will go home and tell their parents not to spray," she says.

She also uses social media to share spider science.

"I do a lot of spider identification through Twitter. This is part of increasing knowledge and alleviating fear," she says. "I love posting photos of the spiders in my garden. People will say they have never seen one before, then, once they are aware say, 'Oh, I have one too!'"

Lizzy also saves spiders by sharing information on moms' groups on Facebook.

"In spring, moms freak out about spiders, because spiders are everywhere," she says. "I respond to posts and say, 'This is my specialty, I can help.' I was expecting pushback, but the vast majority of responses were amazingly positive."

Lizzy found that most of the spiders in photos people shared weren't dangerous. Once she reassured people they were harmless, people chose not to call pest control or use pesticides. People even wanted to know more about spiders, like what Lizzy's favorite one is.

"It's the European cross spider," she says. She has a tattoo of one on her forearm.

Lizzy also does in-person educational workshops for adults.

"I'll meet with probably about 30 interested citizens. They might know about huntsmans or redbacks, but they will be blown away with what I tell them. After, I get a barrage of e-mails, asking for identification, saying I didn't know this, and now I'm not going to spray."

This is exactly what she hopes to hear. Alternatives to chemicals, like keeping food sealed and using small, targeted bait stations, are cheaper and easier, according to Lizzy.

"You don't need flea bombs," she says. "We need knowledge, options, and more regulations."

The regulations would make sure companies don't sell more chemical than people need.

"There's scary evidence cockroaches are becoming immune, like [bacteria are to] antibiotics," she says.

Lizzy also hopes to work more with the pest control industry.

"I've been trying to work with operators," she says. "They get taught how to do six different sprays, but they don't get training in alternate techniques. I want to talk to them and get them to develop education programs. They can offer a new range of product and services that aren't so harmful to the environment. There's a market for this in cities."

Like the threats to spiders and insects, Lizzy is facing threats to her work. Her outreach activities are as essential as her research. But unfortunately, the university only evaluates her research contributions.

"Academia is hard, it's cutthroat," she says. "I'm at the point where I have two young kids and I've stayed afloat thanks to support, but I don't think I can keep it up. I'm being told I have to be top 2 percent to have a job. I'm very good, but I'm not 2 percent. I don't work on weekends, and I don't work at night because I love my kids. I think that's going be why I leave."

Lizzy is experiencing a common threat to women in science. Data show there are fewer and fewer women doing postdoctoral research. And 2020 introduced a new element that makes it even harder for Lizzy to stay in academia: COVID-19 shutdowns.

"Our universities are crumbling," she says. "The university relied a lot on Chinese and Indian students, but we locked our borders in March. That's 40 percent of our income lost. We've basically been gutted."

Universities have had big rounds of redundancies, or job cuts, because of loss of income during the lockdown.

"So many academics have lost their job," Lizzy says. "My job runs out next year. Because I'm early career, I'm at the point where I'd be looking for a permanent lecturing position. But they are actively sacking people instead of hiring. I have other interests, I will be OK. But lots of people aren't."

Again, Lizzy found social media to be a useful resource.

"It's my support group, it's postdocs going through the same things," she says. "I never would have imagined I could have contact with 200 people around the world studying spiders. I ask a question and I get an answer in 10 minutes. It's an amazing resource."

Lizzy feels she can rely on her environmental consultation work and outreach. But she loves working at a university and knows she will miss it if she leaves.

"Doing research is good because you are independent. You devise your questions, you devise how to address them, and you do it," she says.

With so many changes to the academic environment, Lizzy knows she will have to adapt too. Wherever she is, she will continue to work for her goal to be a hero for spiders.

"I've always said to myself it's important to do something that you love," she says. "You have to be true to yourself. You can do something positive. You can make a difference in your tiny little sphere."

Social Media

Twitter: @LizyLowe

Instagram: @learn_to_love_bugs

Part III: Sea Creatures

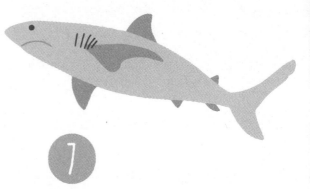

Jasmin Graham: Saving Sawfish and Dodging Shark Teeth

When Jasmin Graham heads out to do fieldwork, she never forgets her boots.

"When we drag sharks up on the deck, sometimes they get bitey-bitey," she says. "They'll go for feet or the sides of boats. One time a lemon shark bit an engine, and there was steering fluid spraying everywhere."

Jasmin is a marine biologist studying smalltooth sawfish. Sawfish look like sharks because they have prominent dorsal fins and long tails, but they are rays. Sawfish also propel themselves with their tails like sharks. But sawfish have gill slits on the bottom of their bodies. Sharks' gill slits are on their sides. Sharks, skates, and rays are all part of a group of animals called elasmobranchs.

Jasmin works in the waters off the coast of Florida in the United States. She works at the Mote Marine Laboratory and Aquarium in Sarasota, Florida. She did research with a team led by Dr. Dean Grubbs from Florida State University, and now she researches in collaboration with Tonya Wiley of Havenworth Coastal Conservation.

Jasmin loves strange-looking animals, and few are stranger looking than the smalltooth sawfish. It has a long rostrum, or saw, that is lined with sharp teeth. It looks like a chainsaw. The sawfish uses this rostrum to find prey.

The smalltooth sawfish is critically endangered. "The major threats are habitat loss and bycatch mortality from commercial fishing. When sawfish get caught in shrimp trawls, they have a high mortality rate, it's basically a death sentence. When they get caught in gill nets, they often don't survive if trapped in the net too long," says Jasmin. "They also get caught in the long line fishery, but that has a high survivability. As long as the people cut the line close to the hook, the sawfish can swim off."

Jasmin is working to identify areas where sawfish spend a lot of time so that policies can be put in place to protect them.

"Scientists have identified three nursery grounds in Florida: Charlotte Harbor, Ten Thousand Islands National Wildlife Refuge, and Everglades National Park. Baby sawfish have protections," says Jasmin. "But when they are six feet (2 m) in length, they swim away. People don't know where they go, what happens to the big ones."

Jasmin studies one of the two main viable populations of sawfish, the one in south Florida. The other population is in the Bahamas. Her research has two main goals.

"We conduct sawfish surveys to see what areas they are using, so that we can hopefully identify critical habitats for the large juveniles and adults in the future," she says.

The second goal is to deal with bycatch mortality. Tracking places where fishing pressure and sawfish activity are at their highest, Jasmin hopes to find a solution that works for fishing and sawfish.

Focusing on these high-traffic intersections can help policy makers find a balance between protecting the economy and protecting species. "Things like just shutting down fishing for a period of time, or limiting the depth of fishing," she says.

For Jasmin, research days start the night before. She gathers needles for taking blood samples. Then she labels hundreds of vials for storing the samples. Next, she checks the three kinds of tags.

"We use dart tags for identification. They are numbered and have a phone number to call if someone catches the fish later," she says. "The satellite tags go on the dorsal fin and float behind them. Whenever they are swimming, it approximates their position based on light, temperature, and depth. After a designated number of days, it pops off and floats to the surface and transmits data to a satellite and we download it."

Last is the acoustic tag. The small black tag is about two inches (5 cm) long. Researchers implant these tags surgically into the fish.

"We sink receivers, they look like cylinders, to the bottom. The acoustic tags send out pings every couple of seconds. Every time an animal swims past a receiver, it registers the pings," she explains.

Then she's up at 5:30 AM the next day loading everything on to the boat.

In summer she wears shorts and an SPF shirt. Sunglasses are essential.

"I do a lot of work in the [Florida] Keys, and the sun is intense. Sunglasses prevent sun burning my eyeballs. I reapply sunscreen a lot," she says. A visor shades her face and has an opening for her hair.

"Before we start fishing, that's my favorite part," Jasmin says. "It's peaceful. The sun is rising, nobody's on the water except for us, you see turtles and dolphins, pelicans, and osprey. The water is clear. It smells like sea salt and the metallic smell of thawing bait. We also use very oily stinky fish, so it smells like fish."

But not every day is beautiful.

"We go out in rain, even if it's raining sideways in sheets, all miserable weather, as long as it's not lightning or winds aren't too strong," Jasmin says. "I've never thrown up, but I have felt icky, had a headache and vertigo."

Shark research means fishing for sharks and usually pulling them onto the boat. Besides boots to protect her feet from sharp shark teeth, another piece of essential gear is her shark-wrangling pants.

"All sharks have dermal denticles [small flat scales shaped like the letter *V*]. Each species has its own shape. Nurse sharks have extremely rough skin—you get shark burn. Theirs can draw blood. You bleed down your arm or leg. It's very exciting," laughs Jasmin.

Every species has its own reaction to being fished out of the water.

"Hammerheads will almost never bite. They are super stressed. They fight to exhaustion on the line, so you don't have to worry about them biting you. They are some of the easiest to handle because they are so tired," Jasmin says.

Hammerheads are very fragile, so the researchers try to get them off the boat within 60 seconds. Nurse sharks are the opposite.

"They store up all of their energy and say 'all right, you've caught me, I'll show you.' As soon as they crack the surface, it's like 'I hate all of you and I'm going to make your life miserable!' They roll and thrash. You put them on the boat, and they will smack the heck out of you with their tails. I have to use my whole body to hold them still for the workup. Usually it takes about three people," Jasmin says.

And all three people should be wearing shark-wrangling pants.

"Blacktip sharks pretend they aren't going to bite you. But as soon as you let your guard down, they are like 'AHA!'" Jasmin says. "But blacknose sharks lay there like limp noodles. Lemons bite everything."

Fishing for sharks has funny moments too.

"I wish there was a blooper reel of people getting smacked around by sharks—it would be hilarious," she says. "A volunteer was pushing a nurse shark off. They always give a last flick. It hit him in the family jewels. His girlfriend couldn't stop laughing. We also have a clip of Dean working on a hammerhead that head-butted him."

But at the end of the day, catching sawfish is the goal.

Sawfish adults can be about 16 feet (5 m) long. They are apex predators and eat small sharks, crustaceans, and bony fish. And they are super intelligent.

The researchers set a long line. Every five or six feet along the line is a shorter line with a hook. The hooks are baited with ladyfish, Spanish mackerel, and bonita. Each line has an anchor at both ends that pull the lines down to the bottom where the sawfish wait.

The scientists check the lines every hour. They usually pull them up with a winch, but if that is broken, they do the hard work of pulling them up by hand.

"When we feel that dead weight, we pull it up really slowly," Jasmin says. "They always come up rostrum first. As soon as you see the rostrum crack the surface, we say, 'Don't let its eye see the surface.' Once it does, it's over. You won't get control."

The researchers first use a tail rope to secure the sawfish.

"They are super strong with giant chainsaws on their face. They swing them super quickly, so we pull them up slowly. We don't want them to panic. We don't want them to realize what's happening," Jasmin says.

The team has to be ready for battle.

"You need good footing, and you have to hold the rope for dear life. A sawfish drags and jerks you. I usually have bruises on my hips," she says. "There are holes in the side of Dean's boat from where they bashed it."

The workups take time, so the researchers hang over the sawfish in the water. They measure the rostrum and count teeth. Each sawfish has a unique and often asymmetrical number of teeth on each side, so they take photos in the hopes of building a photo identification system of sawfish. They draw blood. They secure dart tags, pit tags, and acoustic tags.

"They get all kinds of jewelry," Jasmin says. Then they are released. "We loosen up the tail rope. Then the rostrum rope is moved up a few teeth at a time," she says. "They rarely thrash when they are released. They swim off in a zigzag. They are always so majestic when they swim off."

Jasmin didn't know she could be a marine biologist until high school. She learned about the career at a camp, but her parents weren't sure it was a real job. Jasmin was sure. She graduated from the College of Charleston in 2017 with a degree in marine biology. Initially, she did genetics work to figure out how hammerheads were related to each other. She realized she really liked sharks.

"As an undergrad, I volunteered with the Marine Mammal Stranding Network and realized I wanted to do work that led to real conservation and policy change. I knew I wanted to do conservation and sharks, skates, and rays," she says.

Her mentor suggested she talk to Dr. Dean Grubbs at Florida State University, who was doing sawfish research.

"It had everything I wanted. I like weird animals," Jasmin says. "He got me connected with the Smalltooth Sawfish Recovery Team, a group of people from different fields, academia, government, nonprofit, and fishing on a council that makes decisions about sawfish conservation. I got really involved with that."

There Jasmin met Tonya Wiley, leader of the Smalltooth Sawfish Recovery Team. Jasmin learned about Tonya's work and how she started a summer camp called Coastal Brigades in Galveston, Texas.

"I asked her if I could be her mini-me, and she said yes!" Jasmin says. "It's been great to talk to a woman who's been in science a long time. She cuts through all of the nonsense."

Jasmin is the project coordinator for the MarSci-LACE (Marine Science Laboratory Alliance Center of Excellence) grant. This research program focuses on understanding best practices to support and retain minority students in marine science. This is important to her because Jasmin hasn't had people of color as mentors. She was 21 years old when she first met a Black woman marine scientist at a Smithsonian event in Maryland.

"I remember being in awe, speechless," Jasmin says. "She told me she was 42 the first time she met a Black woman marine scientist."

Jasmin is passionate about sharing her love of shark science. She does Skype-a-Scientist and she was one of four Black marine scientists who founded MISS, Minorities in Shark Sciences.

"We never met each other in person; we found each other on social media through #BlackInNature. We felt like we were alone, but we weren't. We said we should make a club and it spiraled into MISS," Jasmin says.

MISS launched on Juneteenth of 2020. The group has over 200 members from 18 different countries. Its goals are not only to bring people together and make community, but also to provide people with resources and change how shark and marine science operates.

"It's really blown up. It's about providing resources, opening access, and tackling the big bear of systemic issues. There's a lot of people that want to help and want to be on the right side of change. Of course, there are people that don't like change, especially people who are benefiting from its current state. Shark science, unfortunately, is elitist and exclusionary."

Want to Talk to a Scientist?

Sarah McAnulty knows that not all science is done in a lab. That's why Sarah started Skype-a-Scientist, a program that connects the public with working scientists.

"You have these pictures of scientists like kooky White men with crazy hair. And we want people to see that, really, scientists are just regular people," said Sarah.

"Our main goal is connecting as many people as possible with science and scientists," says Sarah. It's clear she hopes these connections will inspire kids.

But another important goal is to overcome a distrust in science held by the public.

"A lot of times people might . . . hear about scientists being funded by corporations and lying to the public," Sarah says. "And if you meet us, you realize it's not really what's going on."

In 2020, there were over 5,000 scientists in the Skype-a-Scientist database.

During the coronavirus pandemic, questions and misinformation made virologists and epidemiologists especially popular. Many kids weren't in schools, and Skype-a-Scientist was available to them in their homes.

One of the biggest issues she tackled were the popular SharkFest and SharkWeek programs from National Geographic and Discovery Channel, respectively. She criticized them in an interview for a blog.

"I'm a very honest person and don't hold back. I said first, Shark Week is rarely about science anymore; now, unfortunately, there's a lot of junk. There are also hardly any women and people of color. They go to all these places and there are never scientists from those places. Why are you flying White American scientists in to talk about research instead of highlighting the local people doing research there already?" she says.

National Geographic responded very positively to her critique and said it would work for change. But Discovery Channel didn't.

"Discovery Channel was supposed to run an article about MISS on their blog, but it never appeared on their social media," Jasmin says. "We followed up and they sent us a link, but they never mentioned it on social media. It was odd."

The Shark Lady

Eugenie Clark was a Japanese American ichthyologist who loved sharks. Born in 1922, she grew up visiting the New York Aquarium in New York City. She entered the field of marine biology during World War II at a time when Americans of Japanese ethnicity were being sent to internment camps, or prison camps.

She did research in Micronesia, including Guam and Palau, as well as the Red Sea off the coast of Egypt. She learned to scuba dive and was one of the few scientists to study living sharks while diving. She named several fish species and has at least five species named after her.

Eugenie founded Cape Haze Marine Laboratory in Sarasota, Florida, in 1955, which is now called the Mote Marine Laboratory. (This is where Jasmin Graham does her work.) Here Eugenie proved it was possible to train sharks.

She made her last dive in June 2014 at the age of 91 and died in 2015.

Jasmin faces prejudice in person too. Out on the water, men on fishing boats will talk to Dean Grubbs but ignore the women on the boat.

"They will ask him questions like, 'You handle the sharks by yourself?' and Dean says, 'There are four other people on this boat.'"

Jasmin is no stranger to bias in the academic community either.

"I've had people try to leverage their power over me. They will ask me questions like I don't know what I'm talking about," she says. "I guarantee I know more about my research than you."

People often ask Jasmin when she knew she was a scientist.

"They think to be a scientist you need to have a PhD or work in a lab. But I was a scientist when I was a kid and didn't know it. I was going through tide pools. I saw this one had a starfish, why didn't others? I tried to figure out which ones didn't. I was doing science," she says. "People can be scientists at very young ages. Undergrads ask me on social media, 'When can I call myself a scientist?' Right now! Claim it!"

Social Media

Website: www.grahamjr.weebly.com

Twitter: @Elasmo_Gal

Podcast: More Than Just a Scientist (https://anchor.fm/mtjas)

MISS website: www.misselasmo.org

Diva Amon:
A Deep Love of the Ocean

There is an unseen, unknown world hidden deep in the ocean full of strange and beautiful creatures. Marine biologist Dr. Diva Amon wants to explore it all.

"Knowing what lives there is the first step because we have no idea," she says.

Diva goes on research cruises around the world. The boats sometimes smell like fish poop and seaweed called sargassum. Sometimes she's in the tropics where the sun beats down hard. Other times she spends hours in a tiny submersible in the cold, dark, deep ocean.

Why does she do it? Because we don't know what's down there. She wants to find out, and she wants to share her findings with people.

"There are spellbindingly beautiful animals down there, and habitats unlike anything else," she says. "But the deep sea has a public relations problem. It's out of sight and out of mind. I wish more people knew about it."

While she's been exploring the depths for over a decade, there are still so many unanswered questions.

"Animals in the deep ocean have pretty weird adaptations. The deep sea is a completely different environment. There is crushing pressure, it's near freezing, and often there's not a lot of food," she says.

She does a lot of mapping and taking photos. What she finds depends on where she is. Just like on land, there are different creatures in different habitats. For instance, creatures like the yeti crab thrive near hydrothermal vents and methane seeps.

"Yeti crabs are white crabs with super hairy arms. Bacteria live in the hairs on their arms. They put their arms in the chemical-rich fluid from the vents and seeps and wave them around. The bacteria feed on the chemicals and multiply. Then the crabs eat the bacteria," Diva says. "They basically have arm farms."

There are also bone-eating zombie worms that eat by dissolving whale and mammal bones that fall to the seafloor. They look like pink and red palm trees.

"One of my favorites in the deep sea is the Dumbo octopus. It has eight arms and two flaps on its head that are actually fins, and it looks just like Dumbo. It's adorable," she says.

The deep sea is full of amazing stories, but few people know about them.

"Science in general is not accessible to everyone, and deep-sea science is the extreme," she says. "Space is the closest analogy. It's incredibly expensive, and only a few nations can do this kind of work."

Diva would love to have the chance to do deep-sea research from her home in the Caribbean, but the cost of this kind of work puts it out of reach for most countries.

"Because of cost, there's only a limited demographic of people involved in this research," she says.

Diva has been on cruises where she was several kinds of "only"—the only person of color, the only woman of color, and the only person from a developing country.

Diva, who identifies as mixed, grew up on the islands of Trinidad and Tobago.

"I spent a lot of time in, on, or around the ocean, snorkeling and sailing. It made me extremely happy," she says. "I have memories of looking down in the water and wondering what was down there."

Growing up in Trinidad, Diva planned to go into medicine. It was one of the few science choices for her to study in her home country.

"But my mother told me to choose something I love, and the ocean was the first thing that came to my mind," she says.

Trinidad and Tobago

The Republic of Trinidad and Tobago is the southernmost nation in the Caribbean. It includes two main islands (Trinidad and Tobago) and 21 smaller islands. The indigenous people are Carib and Arawak Indians. Christopher Columbus landed on Trinidad in 1498. The Spanish settled the island and built the first European villages. The Spanish controlled the islands until the British took over in 1797. The two islands were joined in 1889. The nation gained independence in 1962 and became the Republic of Trinidad and Tobago in 1976.

Enslaved Africans were brought to work on sugar plantations on Trinidad. After slavery was abolished, people from India, China, and the Middle East were brought to Trinidad as indentured laborers.

Modern Trinidad and Tobago is a mix of cultures. People practice many religions, and the largest religious groups are Christians, Hindus, and Muslims. The biggest public holiday celebration is Carnival, and Trinidad and Tobago claim one of the largest in the world.

In 2005, she left Trinidad for the United Kingdom on a national scholarship. She studied at the University of

Southampton at the prestigious National Oceanography Center.

"There were three women who ran courses, but what I found shocking was that in the entirety of my undergrad experience, I could think of one other person who was not White in the building, period," she says. "This is out of several hundred, almost a thousand people. There were no international students. I was the only one, it was really striking."

Diva was lucky to have mentors, including her mother and professors, who supported her. As she progressed through academia, she did seek out mentors who were women.

"I started working with the Deep-Ocean Stewardship Initiative, an expert network founded and run mostly by women," she says. "It wasn't meant to be that way, but women tend to take more of a stand on conservation issues. They are a community that mentored me."

But as Diva continues her research, she admits to feeling lonely.

"There are so few people who have had similar experiences to me," she says. "I always have to carve a path."

Diva is determined to move into areas unknown, like the deep sea she studies. She has been on 17 research cruises around the world.

"I've been fortunate to have worked in the deep ocean of Antarctica, Mariana Trench, the Mid-Atlantic Ridge. I've been really lucky. One of the best parts of the job is getting the chance to travel as part of what you do," she says.

Researching at sea means taking a chunk of the seafloor and bringing it up to the boat. Researchers lower grabs, which are metal boxes with open bottoms, down, down, down into the depths of the ocean. The grabs bring up perfect cubes of the seafloor.

The deep ocean starts below 656 feet (200 m), and Diva's work tends to focus on the areas between 1,500 and 6,000 meters—over 3 miles—deep.

"Don't bring your nice clothes," she says. "You are getting pretty dirty when the samples come on board, there's sediment and animals, so wear the crappiest thing you own."

Diva uses advanced technology to explore the seafloor, like autonomous underwater vehicles, or AUVs. Scientists program the AUVs, and the vehicles descend and take images or gather chemical data. Remotely operated vehicles, or ROVs, are controlled by scientists in real time.

"These are ears, eyes, and hands," she says. "They have cameras, sensors, loads of lights, manipulators to collect samples, and boxes to store samples."

To see the seafloor for herself, Diva uses a submersible. A submersible is like a small submarine that remains connected to the research ship for power or air supply.

"Submersibles are noisy, but when they stop moving, it's almost meditatively quiet. It feels very peaceful," she says. "In the submersible there are no smells. As you surface and watch the sunlight come back and back onboard the ship, the smells hit you. The smell and sunlight remind me of where home is."

Smell and sound are huge pieces of the puzzle that is the deep sea.

"A lot of animals rely on smell heavily because they can't see easily in the darkness. It's a part we haven't even explored yet. There's no easy way to do it, and we can't experience it," she says. "And the sounds of the deep sea are nearly unknown."

A submersible experience lasts nine to ten hours. Which leads to the question, how does one use the bathroom?

"There's no toilet. That for me is always a massive concern," Diva laughs. "They present you with three options. You can use an adult diaper, or you can pee into a contraption called a she-wee, which would mean getting partially naked in a small space with men and women you don't know. The third option is to dehydrate yourself the day before."

Diva chooses the third option. The close quarters of the submersible are just part of the unusual field experience of a research cruise.

"When we go to sea, it's often for a month, and we are far out to sea. There's nowhere to go. It's a really extreme case of fieldwork," she says. "As a result, harassment is a big problem."

Diva has personally experienced harassment and assault on several research cruises.

"I never raised it with anyone, any of the times. Sometimes I wonder if that was the right decision. I didn't seek support. I haven't even told many peers or friends about it."

The harassment usually came at the end of a cruise when alcohol was in play. Diva is grateful she's never had to avoid people at sea and notes a lot of research ships are now dry, or alcohol-free.

Despite these harmful experiences, Diva wants to continue to help people build a connection to the deep ocean. She wants people to care about the unknown creatures. But this is a difficult task.

"It's a lot harder to become endeared to or have those relationships with deep-sea creatures because they look really frickin' weird!" she says. "A lot of them don't have eyes or physical characteristics that cause you to bond with them. Bonds are formed over long periods of observation. That's when you would see it has familial tendencies. But because deep-sea research is so expensive, there are few long-term observations. We don't sit and watch an animal. You go to one place, and no one will go back for tens of years."

Because it is so hard for people to connect, they don't care about the deep sea. This obstacle, and the difficulty of doing deep-sea research, makes it even more important to Diva to speak out for its protection.

"Humankind has not done a good job of preserving or effectively managing the planet," she says. "We are now seeing massive repercussions. We keep hearing about the climate emergency or ecological collapse. This is the final frontier on our planet. We underestimate its importance. We need to change the way we think about our planet and our ocean so we can manage it better and preserve it for generations to come."

"Her Deepness"

Dr. Sylvia Earle isn't a groundbreaking scientist—she's a water-breaking scientist. She is called "Her Deepness" (instead of "Her Highness") for her work exploring the ocean floor. She was the first woman to walk on the deep-ocean floor and the first female chief of the US National Oceanic and Atmospheric Administration. In 1998, *Time* magazine named her the first Hero of the Planet.

In 1970, Sylvia led the first all-woman team to live in Tektite, an underwater installation near the US Virgin Islands, for two weeks. In 1979, she set the women's depth record when she reached 1,250 feet (381 m) deep in a JIM suit off the coast of Oahu. A JIM suit maintains normal atmospheric pressure even in the deep sea.

Sylvia founded a company named Deep Ocean Engineering that creates research submarines capable of diving to 1,000 feet (305 m). She is a leading voice for conservation, and in 2009, she launched Mission Blue with the goal to protect 30 percent of the ocean by 2030. Special places deemed critical to the ocean's health, called Hope Spots, would "save and restore the blue heart of the planet."

Diva has had firsthand encounters with some of the repercussions of human choices even at great depths.

"More often than not, we're exploring a place no one has seen or visited, but we always come across trash or pollution," she says. "One of the most poignant examples was in the Gulf of Mexico in 2017. We drove an ROV toward an unknown target," she says. "Everyone was crammed in the control van, waiting for the first glimpse. Then we saw we were driving through fields of washing machines, fridges, and freezers. A shipping container had ripped open and dumped its contents on the seafloor. It was a part of the planet that *no one* had been to, over 1,500 meters [almost one mile] deep. But it was a field of trash. Definitely one of the saddest and most surreal moments."

The heartbreak of those moments is balanced by the stunning creatures she has found during her research.

"We'd get brittle stars, sea stars, rocks, and corals," she says. "The most amount of coral species live in the deep sea."

And these corals are unlike anything else on the planet.

"Life is very slow in the deep sea. Timescales are totally different because food is limited. Animals conserve their energy.

They move slowly, grow slowly, and get to great ages," she says. "There are black corals that have been aged to over 4,000 years. There are glass sponges, made of silica, that have been aged to over 11,000 years old!"

These ages aren't describing how long the species have been on the planet. These are *individual animals* that are 4,000 and 11,000 years old.

It's startling information.

"Knowing how fragile the deep ocean is, is what I find endearing, and it propels the work I do," she says. "The deep ocean is the largest ecosystem on the planet; it's truly global."

Deep-Sea Mining Damage

Deep-sea mining is just what it sounds like—mining for minerals in the deep ocean. Some of the minerals, like copper, nickel, and cobalt, are needed to produce smartphones and computers. They are also used to create green technologies like wind turbines, solar panels, and electric batteries. Some of the land-based sources of these minerals and metals are getting harder to extract. The demand for these minerals is growing. But deep-sea mining comes with a heavy cost.

According to the International Union for Conservation of Nature, deep-sea mining could wipe out entire species, some not even discovered.

Despite the claims that mining the seafloor would create less waste products than land mining, scientists worry there is still too much unknown about the deep sea.

To save this unknown part of the planet, she uses social media to share what she learns—and loves—about the deep sea. Platforms like Instagram help her reach people outside of the scientific community. This is important to her, because Diva hopes her research will help create strict regulations on deep-sea mining and other harmful activities.

"People working with animals and the environment as important as doctors because they are working on planetary health. I think we should be speaking out about what we're finding."

And there is so much more to discover.

Social Media

Twitter: @DivaAmon

Instagram: @diva_amon

Erin Ashe:
Data, Dolphins, and Whales

It was still dark at 4:00 AM when four-year-old Erin Ashe stood on her aunt's balcony on San Juan Island. Erin listened to the huff and whoosh of killer whales breathing as they swam by in the Pacific Ocean. Those sounds and that moment never left her.

"It lived in my consciousness," says Erin.

Erin is a White American woman. As a child, she loved animals and thought she might become a veterinarian. In 2001, she got her bachelor's degree in science from Western Washington University in the United States. During her time as an undergraduate, Southern Resident killer whales experienced a 20 percent decline in their population size, from a high of 97 whales in 1995 to 79 in 2001.

"I wanted to apply my skills to help in any way I could as I was sorting out what my next steps were professionally," says Erin.

On a postgraduate trip to Argentina, she realized she wanted to be a conservation biologist.

"On the beach at Punta Norte, where killer whales intentionally beach themselves to capture seals, I was struck with fascination and inspiration and knew that I wanted to study wildlife," she says.

She couldn't wait to get back to the San Juan Islands. Erin took on any opportunities she could find to work with marine scientists. She worked two waitressing jobs to pay her bills so she could volunteer on data analysis projects and gain experience. She joined a team to track killer whales from land, and she picked grapes when that didn't pay the bills.

Now, Dr. Erin Ashe is executive director of and a scientist at Oceans Initiative, a nonprofit she founded with her husband, Dr. Rob Williams. They describe Oceans Initiative as "a boundary organization that bridges gaps between science and policy . . . purpose-built to solve societally important problems and shape real-world policy decisions."

"We are team of scientists on a mission to help protect marine wildlife," says Erin. "We do science that will inspire conservation. A lot of our work is an interaction of science and policy. We work on climate change, ocean noise, and fisheries bycatch. We identify if it's a problem and work on mitigation."

Erin researches both killer whales, or orcas, and Pacific white-sided dolphins. She's been studying dolphins for about 10 years, and this project is close to her heart.

"When you encounter them, they're going fast, they blaze through and you don't get a lot of time," she says. "It can be quite exciting. The first time I saw them, it was like looking at an oncoming wall of water. I thought it was a squall—a windstorm that might be too rough for our small boat—but it turned out to be a huge group of dolphins charging through the straits. I was surprised, because all of the field guides I'd read said that this species lived far offshore, and here I was seeing them deep in the fjords of British Columbia."

A population of about 2,000 dolphins has moved into the Broughton Archipelago. This makes it easier for Erin to photograph and study them.

"The archipelago is a beautiful wild complex of fjords and islands," says Erin. "During the summer the dolphins have their babies. You'll find them foraging. They have these neat behaviors to capture schooling fish like herring. But they are also prey for killer whales in that region."

Erin has witnessed a hunting killer whale firsthand.

"One of the first days we were out there photographing, the killer whales had corralled the dolphins into a bay. I saw a killer whale flying through air, and then it killed a dolphin. It was exhilarating and scary. I got a chill. They are serious predators," she says. "I put my dog in the wheelhouse to be safe. It was sad, but scientifically so interesting."

The dolphins didn't always live in the archipelago. They usually prefer the open ocean. But in the 1990s, salmon farmers also worked in this area. Seals moved in to try and feast on the farmed fish. So salmon farmers put up acoustic harassment devices to scare away the seals. But the sounds also scared away the resident porpoises and killer whales.

When the whales and porpoises left, the Pacific white-sided dolphins moved in. They may have been following large schools of pilchards, a kind of fish they like, and just never left.

Scientists can identify individual dolphins by their fins, but in a group this large, it's harder. So Erin now routinely tries to capture photos of uniquely identifiable dolphins swimming in groups of about 500 individuals and then estimates the total population from these samples.

"You have to do math," Erin says.

Math is one of Erin's strengths. She got her master's degree and PhD from the University of St. Andrews in Scotland, learning how to be a quantitative scientist.

"I realized I would love to learn more. I liked the branch of statistics that I applied to photo identification," Erin says.

During her early fieldwork, Erin and her husband lived on a remote island.

"No electricity or running water, only about 400 square feet, only accessible by boat," she says.

She finished up her PhD work right before her daughter was born in 2014. Some things changed. The day after defending her PhD thesis, she pulled down all the sticky notes and to-do lists from her office and turned the room into a nursery. But she and her husband also convinced their supporters to help their nonprofit buy a bigger boat. Erin and Rob now bring their daughter on the water with them.

The Pacific Northwest is cold and often rainy. Erin wears jeans, boots, a fleece, and a hat when doing fieldwork there. She works rain or shine.

"My main scientific equipment is a camera and a field notebook," she says. She knows many younger researchers like phones or iPads, but she prefers written notes.

"If you make a mistake and you're going back through the data, you can double-check," she says. "And the notes can paint a picture, and they tell a story. I have my old muddy and gross ones. They show my progression as a scientist."

In her dolphin research, she's looking at survival rates, how many there are, how their prey influences survival, and how killer whales influence their behavior.

"We watch killer whales from cliffs, but we do dolphin research from a boat," she says. "Up narrow fjords, there are waterfalls, and sometimes dolphins swim under them. We smell the sea air, but there's also a forest smell."

It's clear the dolphins know they are there.

"Sometimes they approach and turn on their side and look up at us," she says.

When dolphins come near, the researchers move the boat slowly or shut down the engine completely. But anyone who has been on the water near dolphins knows they love to bow ride, racing along in the fast-moving water at the front of the boat. They don't seem to appreciate the slow boat.

"It almost looks like younger ones get frustrated," Erin says. "They launch their bodies right in front of us and splash and soak us with water. It does seem deliberate."

Despite the fun of bow-riding, boats do disturb dolphins and killer whales. Like us, dolphins and whales lead busy lives and have specific activity budgets. They spend certain amounts of time traveling, socializing, foraging, resting, and feeding. Boats can disturb foraging time and important socializing time.

"There's a northern resident population of killer whales that lives up near dolphins, and they are the only population in the world that goes to rubbing beaches. These are a series of beaches of smooth pebbles, and the whales rub their bellies along it. It's very social," says Erin. Research shows the resident whales might even host out-of-town family groups who come to visit the beaches.

But the research Erin and her husband publish shows that killer whale activity like this is disrupted by boats.

"We know that resident killer whales are less likely to forage when boats and ships are present, and they stop beach rubbing as soon as a boat approaches," says Erin. "Sound is vitally important to whales. They use sound to communicate with their family, find mates, and find food."

Boat sounds make it hard for whales to communicate with each other. Boat sounds also interfere with echolocation, which is how whales find their food.

To Watch or Not to Watch

Whale watching is incredibly popular. According to a 2008 study by the Whale and Dolphin Conservancy, over 13 million people a year in 120 countries went whale watching. It seems less dangerous than whale hunting, for both people and whales.

But is it?

A BBC article from 2011 stated that "whale watching can have an impact on their natural behaviour, including their ability to feed, rest and rear their young."

In Hawaii, humpback whale populations have made a huge recovery. Whale watching there is less of a problem. But for vulnerable whale populations, like the Southern Resident killer whales, it might be too much of a risk.

"We should use the best available science to make smart decisions now. That probably includes limiting boat number and proximity, from the United States and Canada," says Erin.

There are other ways to watch whales. Erin observes whales from land in her fieldwork, and humpback whales in Hawaii can be seen from numerous places on land. And as the Whale and Dolphin Conservancy points out, watching from land means no chance of getting seasick.

The killer whales Erin studies depend almost entirely on salmon for food. So as human demand for salmon increases, the populations of resident whales suffer. This heartbreaking threat was painfully clear in the media coverage of Tahlequah, a mother killer whale. Her 20-day-old calf died, but Tahlequah carried the calf's carcass on her head for weeks.

Tahlequah and Her Calf

The Southern Resident killer whale population is small—only 74 members divided into three pods named J, K, and L. One member of J pod, whale J35, also known as Tahlequah, captured the hearts of whale lovers around the world.

In July 2018, Tahlequah gave birth to a calf, but her calf died. Tahlequah grieved. She carried her dead calf on her head for 17 days. Members of her pod took turns carrying it for her. She carried her calf while swimming over 1,000 miles (1,609 km).

People around the world grieved with Tahlequah.

Lynda Mapes, an environmental reporter for the *Seattle Times*, has been covering the Southern Resident killer whale population for years. In 2020, Lynda reported that Tahlequah had a new calf, a boy.

While the new calf was welcomed, observers had hoped for a female.

"Southern Resident killer whales are facing extinction unless we buy them time while salmon stocks recover. We need to find ways to build their resilience now to buffer the long-term effects of climate change on salmon," she says. "The population will get smaller and smaller, and you'll lose breeding females and have no functional breeding population. The writing is on the wall, and we need to act now while there is still something left to do."

Southern Resident killer whales are legally listed as endangered.

"We have an obligation to do what we can to help them," Erin says.

The dolphins seem to be doing OK, but no one's really sure.

"We don't have much information. It's hard to study them, and it's expensive, because they are way offshore," she says. "With killer whales, we mourn when the population declines by one and celebrate when there is a new birth. With Pacific white-sided dolphins, the population would have to crash before we knew and could act."

To Erin, data-poor species are a call to action. Erin divides her time between solving the problems we know about and keeping one eye on the problems that may be going on, just beneath the surface.

The Bionic Woman of Good Science

Dr. Jane Lubchenco is nicknamed "The Bionic Woman of Good Science." She believes science can inspire conservation.

Jane is a marine ecologist and environmental scientist. She was the administrator of the National Oceanic and Atmospheric Administration (NOAA) from 2009 to 2013. While at NOAA, she talked about the goal of using science to create policies that worked to protect the environment.

In a 2011 interview, Jane said, "I believe that scientists have an obligation to focus on the most important problems and to share their knowledge broadly. Most scientists focus on publishing in the peer-reviewed literature. In addition to that very important task, it is equally important to get new knowledge into the hands of the public, policy makers, and managers."

Jane hopes policy makers will use scientific information to inform, but not dictate, the difficult choices they have to make. But science needs to be part of the discussion.

Dolphins eat squid, salmon, and herring. Based on Erin's research, it appears dolphins rely on herring as much as salmon for their food—and survival.

"The dolphin project is fundamental ecological research. It can serve as a foundation to learn more about conservation," says Erin.

Erin is no stranger to threats. As a young researcher, she camped in British Columbia along Boat Bay. She heard whales at night again but kept an eye out for bears and cougars.

Being on the water is a risk too.

"It can be scary at times. When we had a small boat, we got into a tricky situation when we came out of an inlet and found a wall of angry seals," she says. "It was getting dark, and I had just found out I was pregnant. We were grateful when we got home."

Like many scientists, Erin faced sexual harassment.

"This one particular time I shared what I was experiencing with another guy on the team, and he was an incredible ally," she said. "I felt like I had an A/B choice: work in this unpleasant situation or have nothing. He was so helpful. He said I shouldn't have to work like this, that what I was experiencing wasn't acceptable. His perspective was what I needed to leave that situation and create a better job for myself."

And like many scientists who have children, Erin was told fieldwork was impossible.

"When I went to Scotland to defend my thesis, I was hugely pregnant. One female colleague said, 'That's it, you'll never do fieldwork again. Say goodbye to that part of your life.'"

But Erin had wildlife scientist Alexandra Morton as a mentor. Erin first met Alexandra in 2003.

"Alexandra raised two children in the field. She lived in the wilderness with her children and studied whales, and I realized I can do that too," Erin said. "I almost took it as a challenge. Maybe it was good that colleague said what she said. It pushed me to think about how I could make it work. I realized we need to identify and celebrate role models, so I started to interview moms in the field."

Virtual Marine Biology Camp

During the COVID-19 lockdown of 2020, Erin and her husband Rob harnessed social media to share their research with Virtual Marine Biology Camp. They created 14 videos on YouTube, a downloadable e-book, and a certificate of completion. Everything is available for free on their website.

Erin and her husband made adjustments, but she is still doing fieldwork and parenting. And she's not the only one. She's collecting their stories to help inform and inspire other scientists.

Through Oceans Initiative, she spearheaded a Women in Marine Mammal Science program.

"This field can attract large personalities, and historically it's been men on boats. Some of the early whale research was from whaling ships, and women weren't allowed," she says.

Erin and colleagues hosted a workshop and sent out a survey to learn about barriers facing women in marine science. She knows there are many different aspects to why there are barriers, and why they are so difficult to overcome.

"We really wanted to identify the challenges and come together as a community to address them and support one another," she says. "Through the nonprofit, we aim to carry that through with opportunities for early-career women."

Erin and Oceans Initiative have been on social media for years.

"Dolphins and whales are so photogenic; Instagram has really been important for the storytelling," she says. "You can share a lot of facts that no one remembers, but they can remember a story. You can reach an audience that will never read scientific journals. We've met so many supporters, people who are really fired up, and we can make great things happen together."

Erin is proud of her unique organization.

"We're doing science, but we're also offering early-career scientists a different experience, and it might even be more challenging. We're scientists in the nonprofit world, and we're entrepreneurial," she says. "We love to work with experts across disciplines to round out a project and ask, Who else can we bring in to help things move forward?"

Social Media

Website: oceansinitiative.org/

Twitter: @OceansResearch and @ErinAshe

Instagram: @OceansInitiative and @ErinAshe

Facebook: Oceans Initiative

Part IV: Reptiles and Amphibians

InvestEGGator:
Turtle Tech to the Rescue

Dr. Helen Pheasey tried to avoid studying turtles. She is a conservation biologist specializing in wildlife trade.

"I didn't want to just work with sexy, charismatic animals," she says. "I wanted to show I was interested in ecology and conservation."

So she studied chameleons in Madagascar, armadillos in Paraguay, small reptiles and amphibians in Indonesia.

But sea turtles are hard to resist, so Helen stopped trying. From 2014 to 2018, she worked in Central America and the Caribbean studying leatherbacks, green sea turtles, hawksbills, and olive ridleys.

A big part of her work involved monitoring nesting turtles. Sea turtles lay eggs during a season. Leatherback season starts in March and runs until the first of June, then the green sea turtle season starts. In April the critically endangered hawksbills arrive. The best time for green sea turtles is August to September.

Turtles laying eggs always follow the same pattern.

"They emerge from the sea and look for a nest spot. They make a body pit and dig the egg chamber. Then they lay the eggs and disguise the nest by violently throwing sand over it and then return to the ocean," Helen says. "Volunteers are always amazed how they use their back flippers like hands."

Turtles don't make a lot of sounds, but they aren't silent. Olive ridley turtles make a drumming sound when they disguise their nests. It's like a dance. During arribadas, or mass egg-laying events, all the turtles drum in unison.

Arribadas

Arribadas is a Spanish word for "arrival." A turtle arribada is a mass, synchronized nesting event. It is an unforgettable sight—and smell.

"There 100,000 turtles at once and it smells really bad," says Dr. Helen Pheasey. "The actual smell is rotting eggs. Turtles are digging up each other's nests and all of the birds are there to predate on eggs, so it also smells like a chicken coop. It's disgusting, and it's inevitable to have egg in your hair."

Only olive ridley and Kemp's ridley turtles form arribadas.

Olive ridleys nest on the Pacific coast of Costa Rica near a town called Ostional. The event has a major impact on the ecology and economy of the town.

Arribadas begin on the darkest nights. Around 150,000 turtles will come ashore and lay up to 10 million eggs. The largest recorded arribada included over 500,000 turtles in November 1995.

And you can hear them breathing.

"Leatherbacks give off a rumbling sound. It's so prehistoric," Helen says. "They are literally dinosaurs. And they are so ugly, like their faces were hit with a shovel."

While the turtle lays eggs, volunteers measure and tag the turtle and count the eggs. It's tough, but they have do this before the turtle covers its nest with sand.

"When a green turtle flings sand straight into your eyes, it hurts," Helen says.

It also hurts to find dead turtles. Poaching for turtle meat, a traditional food, is a problem on Caribbean beaches.

"They take a turtle into vegetation and turn it on its back. It suffocates on its own body weight," Helen says. "If we get there in time, we can turn her over and send her back to the water."

If they get there too late, they find only an empty shell.

"The first time you lose a turtle, you see a drag mark up the beach, morale is low," Helen says. "But it makes us more determined. It's hard work patrolling. People have blisters, walking six hours a night, we're exhausted. But everyone on the team says, 'put me on tonight's patrol.'"

Sea turtle poaching means illegally digging up nests and selling the eggs. Poachers want both turtle meat and eggs.

Exotic Pet Trade

Poaching isn't just stealing eggs or killing animals illegally for food. Poaching can also mean capturing animals and selling them as pets. According to National Geographic, the "illegal wildlife trade is a multimillion-dollar black market."

Social media plays a role in fueling this illegal activity. People use social media to advertise and sell exotic animals illegally. When people shared videos on YouTube of a kind of primate called the slow loris, the demand for these creatures skyrocketed.

Slow lorises are supposed to be protected by the Convention of International Trade in Endangered Species. But the demand for these sensitive, nocturnal creatures makes them a target for illegal pet traders and pushes them even closer to extinction.

Helen is a White British woman. In 2016, she studied turtle egg poaching for her PhD work at the Durrell Institute for

Conservation and Ecology in Canterbury, England. Her field-work was in Central America, on the beaches of Costa Rica.

"We patrolled six hours minimum every night, walking across sand. Our job was to prevent poachers. Just by being on the beach meant we would scare off poachers," she says.

Locals have been eating eggs for decades.

"People who eat the eggs want them within 48 hours of being laid. If a nest was safe for two nights, it was likely safe," she says.

Helen's PhD work included interviewing poachers.

"These are people too. They were so delighted that some-one was talking to them," she says. She got to know the local poachers. They called her "Rasta Girl" because of her long dreadlocks. "I told them in my country, England, if you take food off hedgerows, fruit, mushrooms, it's called foraging, it's cool. Here it's illegal. I'm not here to judge. Why are you doing this?"

On that beach in particular, she learned they were selling the eggs to buy crack cocaine.

"These eggs aren't filling a hunger need; people use them as currency for drugs," she says. "Then you look behind that and see marginalized individuals with low literacy and education and no opportunity to work."

Costa Rica has huge problems with low employment and low income.

"An entire green turtle nest sells for four dollars," she says. "They are not getting a lot of money. Some poachers just had eggs in T-shirts, not even in bags. Poachers sell them door to door, saying '*huevas tortugas*.'"

Helen understood that poachers were struggling. But the threat to sea turtles was real too. To save nests, sometimes Helen and other researchers raced poachers across the beach to get to the nests.

"Whoever got there first and put a stick in the turtle's tracks meant they claimed that turtle. Other people would leave it alone," she says. "But if a poacher was faster than you, you had to suck it up."

In 2018, she learned about InvestEGGator. This innovative program used 3D-printing technology to create fake eggs. The goal was turtle conservation and to reduce poaching of sea turtle eggs. InvestEGGator was created by Kim Williams-Gullen, a conservation scientist at Paso Pacifico. Kim is a White American woman and an adjunct professor at the University of Michigan in environment and sustainability.

Paso Pacifico is a woman-led organization founded in 2005. It provides a space to train and mentor female biologists in Central America. Its members work in Nicaragua and El Salvador, and with partners in Costa Rica and Mexico.

Kim came up with the idea for InvestEGGator. It was a finalist in the Wildlife Crime Tech Challenge in 2015.

"Our very earliest prototype had a transmitter and was casted in a mold with silicone squishy stuff," Kim says.

Another challenge competitor suggested using 3D printing to make the eggs look and feel more realistic. Kim got a used 3D printer and used Ninjaflex, a kind of polyurethane that can be firm or soft. She made the models at home in Detroit, Michigan.

"A lot of model making was done while I was in bed," Kim says. "I'd love to be in Costa Rica all the time, but physically I can't do a lot of travel. I got Lyme disease, and it leaves me partially disabled. I felt very much like I was at the height of my career, and it struck me down. I'm very grateful for these ways I can be involved in fieldwork, and research and development."

Kim and Helen connected. Helen raised money over social media to purchase some decoys.

"They had a prototype ready, I had a beach in mind, and got permission from the Caño Palma Biological Station in Costa Rica to deploy eggs on the beach with the monitor," Helen says.

Kim came to Costa Rica with the fake eggs in an egg carton. They had to program the eggs, but the beach didn't have a great phone signal.

"We walked up and down holding our phones in the air," Helen says. "It was really fiddly and then got really repetitive."

"We tried to be casual about it so that people don't see we're up to something," says Kim.

The spherical, mottled eggs look and feel like turtle eggs. But inside each egg is a SIM card and a charging port. Helen sealed the doors with white paint to make them watertight and less obvious. Then it was time to plant the eggs. They needed to go into nests as the turtles were laying their eggs.

But finding a turtle laying eggs is hard work.

"The whole process of walking the beach in the middle of the night is exhausting," Helen says. "Teams of three people all dressed in black, with no lights at all, walk quietly and calmly up the beach looking for tracks. We'd see tracks coming up the beach, and we would sneak up to vegetation. We're crawling around to find the turtle in the dark. Some nights there's a full moon and it's bliss. There's eye shine from mammals, fireflies going over, the whole thing is so magical, like an enchanted beach. Other times it's pouring rain and you are bumping into everything."

When the research team spotted tracks, they'd move into position and wait for the turtle to be almost done laying eggs before they placed the decoy in the nest.

"If we get it right, turtles don't know we are there, but if they know we are there, they'll scare and go back to sea," Helen says.

They deployed exactly 101 decoy eggs.

"I wasn't sure it was going to work," Kim says.

But most of them did. Sometimes poachers left the fake ones. Sometimes the wiring was loose. But they got meaningful data. Helen received maps via her cell phone app showing where the eggs went, and it wasn't too shocking. Most eggs stayed local.

"We weren't trying to stop the traffickers at this stage," Helen says. "The decoys were only being trialed in the field. No one could be arrested at this stage. Our aims were to see if the devices worked. I just wanted to know what's going on," Kim says. "If you don't know what's happening, you don't know how best to deploy extremely limited resources."

Kim also emphasizes that it was about figuring out who the poachers were.

"If you're a nonprofit working on ground in sea turtle conservation, you know who the local poachers are. It's someone's cousin, and they are financially and socially marginalized in the community," she says. "It's never 'we're gonna get the bad guys' because there's not that many bad guys. It's guys trying to eke out a living."

InvestEGGator was a way to help researchers learn where the eggs were going, and then plan the next steps that would reduce poaching. Since the trackers showed that the eggs stayed local, conservationists could work with rangers and local residents to create awareness programs.

"But if they traveled far away to a big city or big market, you need a different kind of intervention to find those people and mitigate that demand," Kim says—for example, a national campaign to discourage people from eating the eggs. If the eggs went even farther, to other countries, international coordination and education would be necessary.

Turtle Lady of St. Kitts

Dr. Kimberly Stewart is the founder and director of St. Kitts Sea Turtle Monitoring Network (SKSTMN). She dreamed of being a veterinarian and came to St. Kitts from Georgia, United States, in 2002 to study veterinary science. She created the island's first and only turtle conservation organization in 2003.

SKSTMN monitors populations of sea turtles, but it also works for stronger laws protecting sea turtles. SKSTMN studies leatherback, hawksbill, and green turtles. It also offers ecotours to tourists and residents.

Only 1 in 1,000 turtles is estimated to survive to adulthood.

Any strategy includes education as a major component, and that's why education is a huge part of Paso Pacifico's work. The organization focuses on education in their Junior Ranger program for kids ages 8 to 16.

"But we never talked with them about InvestEGGator; it was hush-hush," says Kim. "You need to assess the impacts of using surveillance on your local community."

Junior Rangers do environmental and educational projects like beach cleanups, bird counts, and field activities with visiting scientists.

The Plastic Pollution Problem

In 2018, Dr. Helen Pheasey participated in a PBS News-Hour interview about plastic pollution in the ocean.

According to the report, "forty percent of all plastic, water bottles, bags, straws and utensils are used only one time before being discarded."

The video shows "waves of plastic washing ashore." It's disturbing.

Since 1950, 9 billion metric tons of plastic have been produced around the world. Only a tiny part of this plastic was recycled. Most ends up in landfills and the ocean. It breaks up into smaller pieces, called microplastics.

Birds eat plastic. Fish eat plastic. When we eat fish, we eat the plastic they've eaten.

Sea turtles eat plastic too.

"Single-use plastic is an absolute nightmare for turtles," says Helen. "Up in Florida, they have got a hospital where . . . when a turtle comes in, they no longer say, 'Does the turtle have plastic in its belly'? They now say, 'How much plastic is in the turtle?'"

But the main goal is spreading the message.

"Junior Rangers gets our message of conservation, stewardship, and sustainable use out there," she says. The Junior Rangers in the program also learn scientific skills. They prepare poster presentations and plays. They do wildlife observation and learn about conservation and responsible use.

"But it's not someone coming in from outside saying you shouldn't do that, you should do this. They own it," says Kim.

And as everyone who is invested in protecting turtles hopes, they are passing it on.

Social Media

Dr. Helen Pheasey, Twitter: @HelenPheasey

Caño Palma Biological Station: coterc.org

Dr. Kim Williams-Gullen

Facebook, YouTube, Flickr: PasoPacifico

Twitter, Instagram: @PasoPacifico

Kirsten Hecht: Hellbender Helper

Hellbenders, also known as snot otters, are very unusual-looking creatures. Imagine fat snakes with tiny legs and spotted bodies, glistening with mucous. These amphibians are not the kind of animal that makes the cover of a nature magazine.

But herpetologist Dr. Kirsten Hecht loves them. She used to play with garter snakes growing up. She studies herpetofauna, or "herps," which includes reptiles and amphibians. The word *herpetofauna* means "things that crawl." Her work has focused in the Appalachian region and the Florida Panhandle of the United States. But her work also includes the science of communication, because herps need our help. And Kirsten wants to learn how to help more people love herps.

"People say they have feelings of disgust for these creatures," says Kirsten. "And there are arguments about whether these are innate fears of our animals. This makes it even more difficult to get people interested in conserving them."

What Are Amphibians?

Many people are taught that amphibians "live on land and water." But what about turtles and alligators? They live on land and water too. But they are reptiles, not amphibians.

Amphibians include frogs, toads, salamanders, and newts. Amphibians have thin skin and can breathe and absorb water through their skin.

Another feature unique to amphibians is their life cycle. Some go through metamorphosis. They start as eggs. The eggs hatch into larvae. Amphibian larvae usually live in the water. Think of tadpoles, the larvae of frogs and toads. As they mature, the larvae develop legs and lungs. Some lose their tails. Salamanders and newts don't. Many mature amphibians leave the water and live the rest of their lives on land, but near water.

Amphibians are at risk around the world. In 2008, the International Union for Conservation of Nature (IUCN) listed 1,908 species of amphibians as threatened. Researchers are even more concerned about the lack of information on the 8,000 amphibian species around the world.

It's not just the general public. Kirsten notes there is less scientific funding for herp research too. Confronting this prejudice against reptiles and amphibians is part of Kirsten's PhD work at the University of Florida.

"My PhD focused on learning about how herpetologists engage with the public," she says. "We often do a bad job communicating as scientists and conservationists. We can have all the biology we want, but it's really a people problem."

According to Kirsten, scientists always want to teach, but most adults aren't looking to be taught.

"When you go out and tell people about cool snakes, inevitably people will tell you about snakes they've killed," she says. But if she wants to convince people to help herps, not hate them, she can't get into an argument.

"You can't make a conflict about it. You have to build a relationship with who you are talking with."

One part of her work is focused on learning what works to change people's minds about these species. The second part is how to communicate science, and the third is how to help scientists learn how to communicate with the public.

"Some scientists have learned what works and what hasn't, but it would be nice if they didn't have to learn by trial and error," she says.

Kirsten, a White woman, got her undergraduate degree from The Ohio State University in 2004. She started out as a molecular genetics major.

"Then I realized I was terrible at the lab," she laughs. "I would break things, get burned, hurt myself. It's funny now."

She didn't know ecology was a path she could follow. When she learned about it, she switched and started working with the one herpetologist on campus. Kirsten wanted more field experience, but there were obstacles.

"I came into this field low-income. I went to school on Pell grants. There was a project at the zoo that I wanted to do for research experience, but I didn't have a car, so I couldn't do it," she said. With no undergraduate research, she was behind other students in the field.

"I thought about setting up interviews for master's programs, but felt I wasn't ready," she said.

She did get to do one summer field experience near her home of Sandusky, Ohio. There a teacher asked if she had ever heard of hellbenders. Kirsten hadn't, but she was determined to meet one.

"I was trying so hard to break into this field. But there were so many unpaid internships. Some you even had to pay them!" she says.

Finally in 2005, while working as a cashier, she saw a job hiring for hellbender interns at the Good Zoo in Wheeling, West Virginia. It was unpaid, but the zoo offered free housing.

"When I explained my situation, they got me a part-time job as a janitor. There was so much spilled popcorn," she recalls. "But I was so thankful they understood the issue."

And Kirsten met her first hellbender.

"My very first night an angler brought two in," she says. "I thought, *this thing is HUGE!* It's the weirdest-looking thing," she says. "It never gets old seeing one."

Everyone was worried that one may have swallowed fishing hooks, but X-rays showed it was fine. Kirsten worked with the curator to implant microchips in the hellbenders and released them. That summer Kirsten met even more hellbenders.

"I love that swampy water smell," she says. "We played in milk-chocolatey streams and noodled a lot."

What's noodling?

"Noodling is just sticking your hand under rocks and feeling for hellbenders. They feel squishy. But you try not to disturb the rock because they can slip away," she says. "I had the time of my life."

Herp fieldwork isn't often possible year-round in cooler climates. For some species, fieldwork is only in the spring and summer. Hellbenders go dormant in the late fall and winter, and the water gets cold. So during the downtime, Kirsten returned home to a job at a chain bakery café. But in 2006 she found a paying job with free housing working for a PhD student in West Virginia collecting salamanders.

"At night when it would rain, we'd crawl on our hands and knees up the mountain and catch every single salamander we found," she says. "We'd put numbered flags where we caught them, number the bag, and put the salamanders in plastic bags with water to keep them cool. We'd process them at the station. We'd identify species and hold them up to a light to tell their sex. In some species you can see through their skin and see all their organs. Sometimes you can see the eggs. Then we'd take them back out where we caught them."

This fieldwork experience was in Appalachia. Appalachia is a region in the eastern United States that includes southern New York State down to northern Alabama and Georgia, covering the central portion of the Appalachian Mountains.

"It was coal country. So beautiful, but so much poverty," she said. "Working in Appalachia and seeing the poverty there was hard. I've seen other types of poverty, but in other places there were more resources for people. Here, they were kind, strong, and resilient people, and some lived in shacks covered in billboard paper."

North America Has Amazing Amphibians

Hellbenders are amphibians that are only found in North America. They weigh about five pounds (about 2 kg) and can be almost two and a half feet (74 cm) long. There are only two existing subspecies, found in the wooded streams of Appalachia and a pocket in the Ozark Mountains. People aren't sure where the name *hellbender* came from, but they are also called *Allegheny alligators* and *devil dogs.*

Salamanders are found around the world, but the largest number of different groups is in the United States, specifically, Appalachia. In fact, this region is not only a hot spot for salamander diversity, but also for different types of mussels, freshwater fish, and even crayfish.

"[Appalachia] is a temperate rain forest, so there's new species being discovered there all the time," Kirsten says.

Kirsten is aware of how socioeconomic issues affect people's relationship to the environment.

"Many environmental problems are actually linked to more well-off nations, but the impacts fall largely on communities with fewer resources. Things like sea levels rising from carbon emissions, resource mining for our laptops and phones, and pollution hotspots. Then we often focus on people poaching or clear-cutting to just feed their families and survive."

Kirsten reached out to let local residents know about the study.

"We let them teach us, too," she said.

The second part of the study involved putting flat boards, called *cover boards*, on the forest floor. Then researchers monitored the salamanders that made the cool, moist earth under the board their home.

"Salamanders will stay under them for years. We inject dye under their skin that glows under a black light. It's a little tattoo," she says. "Then you can identify them. We were able to record that one was under the same board for five years!"

It may be surprising that some species of salamanders know who is in their family.

"Some species may have kin recognition, and salamander clans will live near each other," Kirsten says. "We don't know a whole lot about social relationships of salamanders."

Can You Hear Herps?

Some herps make squeaky noises, and the siren salamander makes clicks. Many researchers thought the noises were just accidental, that they happened when salamanders moved. But in one study, scientists recorded the sounds and played them back to other salamanders.

The salamanders responded and reacted to the noises. No one knows what was said, but there is more research to be done in this area.

After Appalachia, Kirsten lived in Panama City, Florida, from 2006 to 2008, and worked for the Florida Fish and Wildlife Conservation Commission. She studied gopher tortoises and looked for an endangered salamander, the flatwoods salamander.

"They asked me in the interview if I would get depressed if I didn't find it," she says. She said she wouldn't, and she and her colleagues never did find the salamander. But the flatwoods salamander isn't gone, and Kirsten has friends working on its recovery. "We did find so many herps, sometimes a little possum, some scorpions, that it was amazing."

Kirsten set up drift fences around ponds so when amphibians came to breed, they had to go around the fences and into traps. She also caught other animals in them.

"There was once a curious cottonmouth on the opposite side of the drift fence, and it came up and checked us out," she says. "We caught a coral snake once in one of our traps. It was clear it had been in and out of the trap. It put its head right up the hole, saying 'I want out.' I don't want to make them human when they aren't, but they are more intelligent than we give them credit for."

Kirsten researched gopher tortoises, native to the southeast United States.

"We did gopher cams. We stuck long cameras down gopher burrows. We'd find crickets, toads, and rattlesnakes," she says. "We'd get to the end of the burrow and the tortoise would be angry and stomping at us."

Gopher tortoises need big open ecosystems, but the lack of wildfires in Florida have let dense forest canopies grow. The canopies kill the underbrush that is their food source.

"Gopher tortoises are a keystone species. Hundreds of species live in their burrows. I never thought I'd find myself recommending clear-cutting and burns."

In 2008, she started her master's degree at the University of Florida. She was back researching hellbender larvae in the Smoky Mountains of Tennessee. Kirsten snorkeled in the clear streams of the Smokies wearing a full-body wetsuit.

"The water is freezing," she says. "But super clear. You can see everything. You pick up a rock and see that hellbender."

She was one of the first people to find out what the larvae were eating and where they live.

"But we still don't know when they leave their nest, or about mate choice," she says.

For many, the next step would be to get a PhD. But Kirsten's path through science has been as unique as the creatures she studies.

"When I started my master's degree, I got unexpectedly pregnant," she says. "I remember a woman professor saying, 'You have to choose between having a family and being a scientist.' I was feeling terrified and conflicted," she says. "Once you have a kid and if you try to be a scientist, you're the exception. I didn't want to tell my advisor at the time, who was a man. I hid it for six months."

Luckily, when she did tell her advisor, he was supportive. But she still needed help.

"After I separated from my husband, my mom used to come and help me care for my son," she says.

She completed her master's and then took a few years off. But she missed studying salamanders. In 2013, she was ready to pursue her PhD, but then her mom got cancer.

"It wasn't safe for me to take my son into the field alone, and then I was dealing with grief from my mother's passing," she says. She wanted to return to studying her beloved salamanders, but she also found that understanding the psychology of science communication intrigued her too. She was torn between following these two paths. Then she got some advice from a mentor.

"She told me, 'You don't have to choose. You can do biology and social science and put them together.' It blew my mind," she says.

Her prior experience communicating with the public and local residents was a key part of her research.

"Hunters out in the panhandle have a lot of knowledge. We may not always agree on everything, but they can teach you a lot," she says. "There are examples of people in other areas reporting more animals in one summer than the state biologists had found. Part of the reason I went into engagement research is to help teach other scientists how to include locals as well."

Communication with local residents isn't always easy. The Florida Panhandle was a good place for her to learn this.

"Locals called salamanders *puppy dogs* and *spring lizards*," she says. "If I said I was hunting salamanders, they thought I was hunting pocket gophers, because gophers build mounds that were called s*andmounders*, which became *salamanders*. It was an important lesson in communications."

Kirsten respects locals. But that doesn't mean she always gets respect as a female scientist.

"I remember being in my work truck in my uniform and someone stopped and kept asking me if I was OK, was I lost, was something wrong with my truck? I'd tell them, no, I'm just doing my job," she says. "Seeing a woman interested in the animals I'm interested in brings up interesting dynamics. Girls are told they shouldn't like these kinds of things. But you can like what you like."

Kirsten feels her biggest barrier has come from being a single parent in academia. And she is not alone in this.

"I did a lot of student advocacy work and got so many e-mails from people saying they are pregnant and scared to tell their advisor. Student parents don't count as an underrepresented group," she says. "We're an invisible demographic. I'm a single parent, low-income, and it's taken me longer to do things. But that doesn't mean that I'm not good at it."

Being a single parent scientist makes it tough for Kirsten to advance her career. She worries that this helps perpetuate the false stereotype that moms can't be good scientists.

"Trying to get to conferences is a hustle," she says. "I'm already poor, living off one income. I like how the Partners in Amphibian and Reptile Conservation (PARC) does regional meetings at state parks, so cost is low. I apply for grants and help with the event. Friends let me bunk in rooms or give me rides."

It was this support from her friends that inspired one of Kirsten's claims to fame. On the way to a conference in 2016, she came up with her wildly popular hashtag, #HERpers.

"We suddenly realized everyone in the van was a woman. We were a herpetology girl gang going to a conference! At a rest area we took a photo, and I wanted a bad pun hashtag, and I came up with #HERpers. I said on Twitter, 'I know we all work hard, show us your field pictures,' and it took off. It was on Buzzfeed. It was so nice to be in something celebrating us."

Along with fellow team members at PARC, she also started the Twitter account @HerpetALLogy, which supports making herpetology more inclusive.

"My biology research is important, but this kind of work helps move the field forward," she says.

An Early HERper

Bertha Lutz was a herpetologist and a feminist from Brazil. Born in 1894, she studied natural sciences and biology at the Sorbonne in Paris, France. She returned to Brazil in 1919 and was politically active. She was a delegate to the

United Nations founding conference in 1945 and signed the UN charter. She fought for women's right to vote in Brazil, which was granted in 1931.

Bertha specialized in poison dart frogs. Three frog species (amphibians) and two lizards (not amphibians) species are named after her. She died in 1976.

When Kirsten first began her PhD work, she wasn't sure it would all fit together. "Now it does. My fieldwork is getting the information about animals to help conserve them. My other work is about engaging with the public so they can get involved in solving conservation issues. Focusing on the human side of conservation has changed my whole career. When people are asked to participate instead of told what to do, they get involved more. This is the future of conservation."

Social Media

Website: kirstenhecht.com

Twitter: @HellbenderHecht

12

Sneha Dharwadkhar: Research in a Herpetology Hot Spot

Like most herpetologists, Sneha Dharwadkhar's fieldwork begins when the sun goes down. She heads out into the forests of the Western Ghats, a mountain range in southwest India.

"At night the forest becomes alive," says Sneha. "It's vibrant. White flowers that flower only at night. Insects calling, frogs calling, moths flying. It's a whole different place, one that I love."

As a herpetologist, she's looking for amphibians and reptiles, also called herpetofauna. One of her main goals is to count the number of individuals and species present in an area and their geographical location.

But hunting for herps isn't all frog calls and flowers.

"If you are in wet areas in the rain forest, you need leech socks," she says. "You wear them over your pants and tie them very tightly around your knee. Otherwise, the leeches would enter your pants."

Sneha uses all her senses in the field, but some are stronger than others.

"I'm really bad at frog calls," she says. "But I have a really good sense of smell."

Sneha uses her sense of smell to stay aware of herbivores in the area. Elephants can be especially dangerous.

"My field collaborators taught me how to look for signs of elephants," she says. "It's a survival technique. If you startle them, they may get afraid and attack."

Sneha is interested in all kinds of herps. Luckily, India is a hot spot in terms of biodiversity. The Western Ghats span several states in India and are one of the hottest biodiversity hot spots in the world.

Western Ghats

While the Himalayas tower near the northeast border of India, the Western Ghats are the opposite. These low grass-covered mountains roll along the west coast of India.

The Western Ghats are listed as one of the eight hottest biodiversity hot spots in the world, according to UNESCO, the United Nations Educational, Scientific, and Cultural Organization.

Some species are endemic, meaning they live only there and nowhere else in the world, including plants, insects, and herps.

The Critical Ecosystem Partnership Fund (CEPF) reports that "Approximately 157 species of reptiles are reported from the Western Ghats. Of these, nearly 50 percent are endemic . . . Endemism is also high among lizards (65 percent)."

This region faces threats from plantations for growing tea, coffee, rubber, and palm oil. Clearing land for roads, livestock grazing, and cities has destroyed habitat. Poaching and "human–wildlife conflict" also threaten the region, according to the World Wildlife Fund.

But CEPF notes that there is very little known about the region, which makes conservation extra challenging.

For Sneha, when she finds a herp it's look, don't touch.

"I use visual encounter surveys; they are the least destructive," she says. A visual encounter survey means only counting the animals you see, not hunting and capturing. She uses a white LED Fenix torch, or flashlight.

"I don't like catching animals," she says. "I'm not blaming anyone. But if I can identify an animal by looking at it, I won't catch it."

It's not that she doesn't want to touch these creatures. On the contrary, she enjoys handling animals she likes. But she has scientific concerns about it.

"I am very touch sensitive. If I like an animal, I want to touch it. But amphibians are very sensitive. They breathe through their skin. If I am touching one frog then touching another, I could be transmitting an agent of disease from one to another."

She won't even lift up logs or rocks, if it's not necessary.

"I don't prefer disturbing the microhabitats," she says.

Her concern for her study subjects is codified in law.

"In the Indian Wildlife Protection Act, if you don't have handling permits, you can only see them, you can't catch the animals."

Sneha is from Vadodara city in Gujarat. Sneha does her work in Maharashtra, a state on the west coast. She speaks several languages, including Gujarati, Marati, Hindi, Tamil, and English.

Growing up, Sneha planned to be a psychiatrist. Although she did well in school, her grades weren't good enough for medical school. She was a city kid and didn't have a lot of exposure to animals beyond dogs, cats, goats, and cows, but she was fond of them. She had always loved visiting her grandfather's garden, so when she saw an advertisement for an entrance exam to environmental science, she registered.

"I topped it," she said, meaning she scored the highest grade on the test.

There are no government loans for students in India, but Sneha's father agreed to pay for her fees. While she studied, Sneha also volunteered with a local rescue group.

"That's where I was introduced to snakes and crocodiles," she says.

Her favorite animal is a particular species of crocodile called the Marsh crocodile. These crocodiles are at home in her city. When monsoons hit, the crocs leave the river and end up everywhere from park benches to people's homes. Her city is famous for it, and residents are used to it. They call the forest department or a rescue organization to remove them.

"When I go for my morning runs, I can stand on a bridge over the small river and see a Marsh crocodile," she says. Unfortunately, the river is very polluted.

"It's like a gutter, it's filthy," she says. "But they have made it their home. They are thriving. Their resilience is incredible."

Marsh crocodiles are also called Mugger crocodiles. Sneha handled them during rescues. One crocodile, about two and half feet (1 m) long, made an unforgettable impression.

"It whipped its tail on my back. The slap mark was there like a week," Sneha recalls.

Muggers average 10 feet (3 m) long. They're not just big, they're smart too. If you lay a trap and they find a way to escape, they will never go into a trap again. But they rarely have trouble with people.

"There are some conflicts when they are nesting, if a person comes too close to a den," says Sneha. "There are some instances where a crocodile has killed people, very rare."

Sneha tries not to handle venomous snakes. But she has been bitten by nonvenomous ones occasionally, especially during her initial training of handling snakes.

"They bite in self-defense, for instance, if you were mishandling it or the snake was stressed. It's not a badge of honor," she says.

Sneha loves crocodiles and other herps, but her main project is researching freshwater turtles and tortoises. She is the co-founder, along with Anuja Mital, of Freshwater Turtles and Tortoises of India (FTTI).

"India has 29 species of freshwater turtles and tortoises, but people don't know there are so many. Most think of sea turtles," she says. "But in the state of Assam there are 19–20 freshwater species in one region. That's the turtle hot spot of maximum diversity in one single region."

Sneha researches the Leith's softshell turtle. This turtle is large and grows up to 31 inches (80 cm) across. It has an orangish head, but despite this feature, it is hard to spot. So she turns to people who know the area.

"I ask the fishing community," she says. "I love talking to the people. They have very little, but they open their homes. I am lucky to be in this field where I meet very different kinds of people."

She shares photos of the turtles with the locals.

"The regional names of the Leith's softshell turtle are different in different states," she says. "So I carry pictures of the turtles of that region along with the pictures of some turtles not present in the region to get accurate information."

Once Sneha knows these turtles are in an area, she looks for basking spots. But she has to be sneaky—and fast.

"If they spot you, they will dive in the water. They are way faster than you," she says. "Sometimes there's the sound of plopping and you say, 'Oh no, a turtle!'"

Who knew you had to be so quick to catch a turtle?

There is very little known about Leith's softshell turtles. Sneha is dedicated to learning all she can.

"What I want to do is find the population, what it eats, where does it live, where does it roost, when is it active? We don't know!"

Eventually Sneha hopes to snorkel in the river and see the turtles in their habitat.

"A major threat is habitat loss," she says. "If you dam the river and cut down the habitat, you will affect prey. It's carnivorous, it eats fishes, mollusks, and arthropods, so understanding species ecology means understanding what you need to protect."

Sneha worries that a lot of turtle conservation, like artificial hatcheries and focusing on eggs, isn't effective.

"It's short-sighted conservation," she explains. "You are only looking at a very short-term goal. If you're not looking at the larger picture, the species is not benefiting. It's only that you are feeling good about protecting it." Sneha also knows regional and indigenous communities need to have a role for truly effective conservation.

What Is the Red List?

The Red List is a complete list of animal, plant, and fungal species. It indicates which are faring well and which are facing extinction in our world. The official name is the Red List of Threatened Species. It was created by the International Union for Conservation of Nature (IUCN) in 1964.

The IUCN describes the Red List as a "critical indicator of the health of the world's biodiversity."

It helps scientists predict which species face extreme danger and where there are chances to help.

The Red List includes some success stories, like the Grand Cayman blue iguana. Protecting habitat and educating people helped move this species from Critically Endangered status in 1996 to Endangered in 2012.

But more often, the Red List highlights the decreasing biodiversity around the world. According to the current list, "there are more than 128,500 species on The IUCN Red List, with more than 35,500 species threatened with extinction, including 40% of amphibians, 34% of conifers, 33% of reef building corals, 26% of mammals and 14% of birds."

Because she couldn't do fieldwork during the COVID-19 lockdown, Sneha and her colleague focused on recruiting local community scientists to help with turtle identification.

"There are a lot of wildlife enthusiasts and amazing photographers," she says. "Pictures are a very important data source."

Sneha found social media to be an especially valuable resource for FTTI.

"I started social media accounts for it, and the project really took off. People started noticing. While they were stuck at home, they were going through their archives and uploading photos," she says. Sneha and Anuja also started posting educational content.

Community scientists uploaded their photos to the India Biodiversity Portal (www.indiabiodiversity.org). In addition to the photo, they share the location and the date and time of the photo. Sneha and Anuja are writing up their research from these photos and hope to publish it in 2021.

Sneha has also written about women in herpetology in India, how many there are, and what challenges they face.

"We are in a field that is considered macho," she says. "People think of crocodiles and snakes. There are 50 million snake bites in India each year. So many women do snake bite education programs. And herpetology isn't just going out and catching animals. It's also spending time in a lab. A lot of it is writing."

There are a lot of Indian women in conservation and wildlife, but Sneha didn't have a female mentor in terms of research.

"During my earlier days in this field, I didn't have a female mentor to look up to, as my role model," Sneha says. "The reason why I and my colleague started FTTI is to provide a platform where we can collaborate with other people who have done research but also for young people, especially young women who want to study in this field. We are just beginning. We hope it will be a platform for people who want to engage in freshwater ecology."

In addition to building an in-person community in India, Sneha found another community through Twitter.

"Two to three years ago when I first got active in Twitter, hardly anyone was tweeting about Indian herpetology," she says. "Now there are a lot of herpetologists from India on Twitter, but I was one of the first. Everything I was putting out was getting a lot of attention, because no one knew a lot about

India. Herpetologists love looking at animals from different countries, and it was cool to share with them."

Sneha made friends, found collaborators, and even got references for graduate school applications through Twitter.

While Twitter has helped her professional career, Sneha uses Instagram for her personal stories and activism.

"There are a lot of papers being shared, new research, podcasts. That's increased my understanding and added to my knowledge. Everyone was so nice to me, everyone was always promoting me. I used to get a little scared, even when I would write something, there were so many typos, now I have come to terms with it," she laughs.

Sneha found it difficult working in northern India.

"There was a lack of toilets and I had to go out in the open, and that got me health infections," she says. "But it was most difficult in terms of safety, going out as a woman, there was a constant threat of something will happen to me. It weighed on me heavily. I kept thinking, *you're not safe, you're not safe.*"

Concerns about her safety limited the time she could do fieldwork.

"One of the reasons I stopped working in north India was that it is impossible for a woman to carry out fieldwork at night. A lot of my fieldwork was in the morning, in the states of Uttar Pradesh and Madhya Pradesh, along the river Chambal."

She returned home and resumed her work in Gujarat. Despite these threats to her personal safety, Sneha feels lucky to be able to follow her chosen path.

"I think my independent streak has been there since I was a child. I almost raised myself and my sister. Our financial situation was not great because both parents were working to make ends meet," she says.

Sneha is also an educator and works with young people as a part of FTTI. But as much as she teaches young people, she learns from them.

"They are inspiring. They come with fresh ideas and their questions bring you back to reality," she says.

And Sneha is committed to supporting young people.

"As a child I didn't grow up with privilege, so I consider being able to make a difference a privilege," she says. "I've seen people who've had a bad past, they've become bitter. This ability to give and receive love, especially to young children, it's a privilege that I am blessed with. Being in a field I love, I will always help young women. I'm going to be there for them."

Social Media

Twitter: @herpomania and @Fttfindia

Instagram: @herpomania and @fttfindia

Facebook: Freshwater Turtles and Tortoises of India

Part V: Mammals

Asia Murphy: Carnivores on Camera

Over the summer of 2020, Asia Murphy played peekaboo with a rattlesnake.

"My goal was to get pictures of baby rattlesnakes," explains Asia. "But I needed to find a basking site. I found one site with three pregnant rattlesnakes. I'd come back every week or so and check on them because the babies only stick around for 10 days."

On one visit, she only saw two snakes. Where was the third?

"I stepped on a flat rock and heard a soft hiss. I saw a yellow head poking out from about two feet away. For about two minutes, we played peekaboo. She'd poke her head out and taste the air to see if I was gone. I stayed to get photos. It was fun. Snakes are really polite. I really like them."

Asia is a graduate student at Penn State working toward her PhD in ecology. She goes by the nickname "that Black camera trap queen" on Twitter. She loves photographing all kinds of carnivores, but her current camera trap research focuses on taking photos of fawns, or baby deer, in Pennsylvania. Asia looks at photos of fawns and uses their spot patterns to count how many fawns are in an area and which fawns survive the summer. The Pennsylvania Game Commission funds her research. The commission is concerned that coyotes are eating all the fawns.

Camera Traps

Camera traps don't trap animals—they snap photos of wildlife. The cameras are motion activated. When an animal creeps past, a bird flies by, or even a bug zooms past, the camera takes a photo. Camera trap equipment is a camera inside a strong plastic or metal box covered in camouflage.

Asia had 100 cameras spread out over 356 locations for her dissertation project. She collected about 100,000 photos. There is artificial intelligence that can look at photos and recognize animals, but Asia likes to do it herself.

"Sometimes you get to see things that you wouldn't normally. Also, it's kind of like a fun scavenger hunt," she says.

Camera traps keep humans out of the picture as much as possible. And they are less stressful for animals than many other forms of observation or tracking.

"Animals will hear the click of the camera and see the light from the flash," says Asia. Animals might smell or move cameras but rarely damage them.

"I do have a video of a bear trying to chew one," she says. Luckily, the metal box protected the camera.

While Asia focuses on fawns, it's really carnivores like coyotes that have captured her interest.

"Fawns avoid predators by staying away from where coyotes are in space, and when coyotes are active in time. This is how species coexist."

Asia expects her research to show that when humans destroy habitat, there isn't enough space for species to give each other space.

"Humans are like a loud, kinda selfish roommate. By figuring out how our actions change the behavior of our roommates (wildlife), and what kind of trouble we give them, we can work on doing better."

In addition to coyotes, she's interested in small carnivores like weasels, wolverines, and civets.

"They are really fierce for their body size and super dangerous. No one is really studying them. I would be one of the first people to get information on them," she says.

Asia is often on her own during her fieldwork. She hates that. She's worried about bears, but they aren't her biggest fear.

"I've gotten interested in how you avoid being killed. Prey creatures usually take in presence cues, smells, sound, sight. I relate that to being a Black woman. I do the same thing. What do I see? A Confederate flag, MAGA hat, hearing the *n*-word," she says. "Out of any species, humans are the most feared."

Asia didn't dream of being a camera trapper while growing up in Sacramento, California.

"I knew I wanted to do something with wildlife. I grew up reading *National Geographic* magazines and *ZooKids* books," says Asia.

Her first real experience working with animals was volunteering at the Sacramento Zoo when she was 16.

"When you volunteer at a zoo, you learn quickly if this is for you or not," she remembers. "I worked with a number of animals. I cleaned up the primate house, which I hated."

Then she had her first up-close carnivore encounter with a hyena.

"She was an old female in her cage. I was power washing her enclosure. At first she was lying down, but she got up when I was done and sniffed around. I never realized how big they were. Her head was up to my chest," she says.

Asia studied fisheries and wildlife at North Carolina State University in the fall of 2008. She was the only Black undergraduate student in her program for three years.

"I did feel out of place, and like I couldn't really make friends," Asia says. By her sophomore year, she was tired of the program. She didn't like her classes. She thought about switching majors.

Then, through a mentorship program, she met Nyeema Harris, a biology PhD student.

"Without Nyeema, I would not be where I am," says Asia.

Nyeema encouraged Asia to do fieldwork. Asia's first experience was a paid position in the summer of 2010 trapping small mammals on the Minnesota prairie.

"I hated it," Asia remembers with a laugh. "There were a whole bunch of ticks. And I didn't like the small town. It felt like I was the only Black person there."

But the mammals were super cute. And the research?

"It was a spark. Just being able to be outside, learning how research worked, I knew I wanted to get into the field," says Asia. "But I didn't know how."

But she did know Nyeema. In 2011, Nyeema introduced Asia to Dr. Marcella Kelly, a population researcher renowned for her work in conservation biology. Dr. Kelly introduced Asia to camera trapping.

Dr. Marcella Kelly

Dr. Marcella Kelly may be the first female camera trapper project lead ever. In 1999, she heard about camera trapping research on tigers. She wanted to try camera trapping jaguars in Belize. She started with a small grant, 15 cameras, and a lot of doubt.

"We hardly ever saw jaguars. I thought, *it's not going to work*," she says. But when the film was developed—jackpot. "There were five individual jaguars at that one station. I thought, *Oh my god, this is actually working! I need to get more money!* I couldn't sleep for a couple of days."

Now she has five study sites in Belize and hundreds of cameras.

"There were so many obstacles," she says. "I was told 'it's too hard, it's too far, there are no trails, no roads.' I thought, *Oh, I can't.* But I finally decided to do it. I went into the forest with my machete and a field helper, often my husband. Then a couple of guys from the research station joined me. They saw me doing it and said, 'Oh, I guess you can.' That's the way I've approached it ever since. When someone says no, don't believe it. Just try. It can lead to great things."

That summer, Asia worked for Dr. Kelly in a camera trapping program in southwestern Virginia. She was hooked.

"If you trap a bear, you're not seeing it as it would naturally behave. The camera helps you see it doing its thing," she says.

Asia wanted to keep doing research, but she needed money. She won a National Science Foundation Grant in the fall of 2011. Marcella suggested doing work in Madagascar.

"As soon as she said that I was like 'OH YEAH.' I didn't need to know anymore," says Asia. She headed to Madagascar in June 2012—the middle of winter.

"I hated it," Asia says, again laughing. "I thought Madagascar was tropical and that it would be warm and dry. It was cold all the time."

The field site was a six-hour hike through the rain forest.

"We went uphill, downhill, in the mud. I tripped and fell a lot," she says. Being at the field site wasn't much better.

"It smelled like mold, especially in the tent. It rained. You couldn't get dry."

And most of the animals were laying low.

"But not the leeches. There were a lot of leeches. Basically, a worse version of ticks."

After a week, Asia got sick. It was a bad cold, but she headed back to the capital city, Antananarivo. There, something she ate or drank gave her a parasite. She had vomiting and diarrhea for three days.

This was especially difficult for Asia as she has had Crohn's disease since she was 11. Crohn's disease is a kind of inflammatory bowel disease. People with Crohn's experience stomach pain, fever, rashes, joint pain, and more.

"I've been in and out of the hospital since I was a kid. Lot of medicines, lots of times when I had to give myself shots. I go to the hospital every two months to get shots."

Once Asia got home, the other researchers said she didn't have to go back. She could study the photos that other researchers had already taken.

"Maybe it was a mixture of stubbornness or anger, maybe a sense if I didn't make it, I wouldn't do what I wanted, so I decided, 'I'm gonna go back.'"

Asia went back in July 2013. She loved it. She stayed for six months until January 2014.

"I was there on the cusp of spring. It was rainy and cold for the first month," Asia says. "but Mangabe in late spring is really nice. There's fruit ripening, like lychees and pineapple. It's still raining, but it's warmer and the sun will come out and you can get dry."

She worked several field sites. The Madagascar surveys had 24 locations, with one or two cameras per location, so 24–36 cameras total. Every day her team pulled photos of Madagascar crested ibis, as well as striped civets, ring-tailed vontsira, and fossa (three catlike relatives to the mongoose). Her favorites were the beautiful fossa and the dramatic crested ibises.

Things weren't easy, but they weren't as hard as before. The sunrise songs of lemurs helped.

"The best part was the indri, these giant black-and-white lemurs. Every morning they sing around 5:00 AM. It sounds like whales."

But it wasn't perfect. According to Global Forest Watch, Madagascar lost about 20 percent of its tree cover between 2001 and 2018. Most of the disappearing forest became farmland.

"Coming to a forest clearing that was supposed to be rain forest, it was a shock," says Asia.

She misses Madagascar, but there are other places she wants to research carnivores.

"I would like to do surveys in Southeast Asia. Everybody's focused on clouded leopards and tigers. But there are 12 species of weasels, mongoose, and civet, and they are seed dispersers and predators, so they are important too. No one's looking at them, because the bigger ones got all the attention."

In addition to her PhD work, she's helped young people learn about conservation and ecology. She has worked with the Philadelphia Zoo Crew and organized field excursions.

"I've taught some people how to camera trap. I've also Skyped with elementary schools through Skype-a-Scientist and narrated battles for March Mammal Madness created by Dr. Katie Hinde."

Asia uses the power of social media when it comes to sharing her research. She tweets about her doctoral research using #WhosEatingBambi. For her next research project, she plans to use #DarkForestDarkCity. In this project, she and her fellow researcher will use camera traps to examine how human light and sounds affect local species in urban areas.

"I think I'll be seeing a lot of raccoons, opossums, skunks, animals that are adapted to cities. I hope to get pictures of coyotes!" says Asia.

She hopes to mentor Black, Indigenous, people of color (BIPOC) undergraduates at University of California, Santa Cruz and donate some of her equipment to Oakland and San Jose public school science classes to supplement their education.

Asia is one of very few Black women doing camera trap work.

"I know I wasn't the first person to use camera trap data to study other species, but I was first in Dr. Marcella Kelly's lab. As one of the unicorns in the field, I have made it my mission to interest as many BIPOC youth in ecology. I've learned there's a value in being visible, especially if you're a Black researcher in this field, it's hard to picture what you don't see."

Looking at the overlooked is her signature.

Social Media

Website: https://asiajmurphy.com

Twitter: @am_anatiala

Instagram: am.anatiala

14

Tatjana Rosen: Secret Cats of Central Asia

In September 2019, Tatjana Rosen returned to her campsite in Turkmenistan. She was only 12.4 miles (20 km) outside the capital city of Ashgabat, in an area called Dushak Erek Dag. Steep canyons carved through the dry mountain landscape.

She found a surprise waiting for her outside her tent.

It was a paw print—a big one, and it was fresh.

"There was a Persian leopard paw print. It was so symbolic, like coming to say hello," she says. "I am trying to learn more about imperiled cat species. They are most dear to my heart."

Persian leopards live in the Dushak Erek Dag. They hunt the sheep and goats. Persian leopards are quiet, secretive creatures. They can live in places without people even knowing they are there. In fact, Tatjana has never seen one in person.

"One time I heard it. They make this very loud grunting noise when they are marking a site," she says. "It's the most amazing sound. I should be terrified. For some odd reason, I feel alive. You feel like you are in the presence of something incredible."

Tatjana studies numerous cat species, including snow leopards, the Asiatic cheetah, and the little-known Persian leopard. Persian leopards are a subspecies of leopard. They are the biggest leopards, even bigger than African leopards, and they are solitary creatures. Mothers raise one to three cubs a year. Persian leopards and Amur leopards are the most endangered of the leopards.

There isn't a lot of research on the Persian leopard. It lives in the Caucasus and Central Asia. This includes countries like Iran, Azerbaijan, Armenia, Georgia, and Turkmenistan.

"It inhabits countries that are poorly known and incredibly misunderstood," says Tatjana. "The biggest population is in Iran, maybe 500 to 600 animals, and the nature and wildlife there is not well appreciated by the international community."

There are also about 50 to 60 Persian leopards in Turkmenistan, where Tatjana works.

"It is a very closed country, politically, there is very little contact with international organizations," she says. "In 2018, we embarked on this effort to understand where the leopards are and how many."

Tatjana and her colleagues use camera traps to identify and count the number of individual leopards in an area.

"We spend important moments in the capital discussing our findings, but our real work is in the field, looking for places to put the cameras," says Tatjana.

In Turkmenistan, she stays in the field about two weeks at a time.

"Because of the country, there [are] limitations, we have to report back to the capital every two weeks. Being a foreigner, even if you are trusted, it comes with additional concerns," she says. "They really care about the safety of foreigners, like if I were to break an arm, it would be very upsetting for [the] government. It would be translated as we didn't take good care of you."

Photographs are essential to her study. Like many cat species, individuals can be identified by their unique spot patterns. But she doesn't have enough cameras. So Tatjana also identifies the cats by what they leave behind.

"We have been collecting their scat, or poop, and [have] taken samples to a lab in Germany," she says. "That process of collecting data is complementary and compares with what we think we have based on camera traps."

Even with all these challenges, her work in this region has led to exciting new discoveries.

"We cooperate with a team in Kazakhstan, and for the first time a Persian leopard was detected on camera traps there," she says. "We tried to understand where this leopard came from and surveyed a small mountain area in the northwest part of Turkmenistan. We found five to six individual Persian leopards."

And she has found evidence about more cat species beyond the Persian leopard.

"The Persian leopard is a flagship to understand lesser-known species," Tatjana says. "The Pallas's cat was never recorded on camera traps, in one year we saw three different individuals in two areas. We recorded the caracal for first time on camera trap. Also a striped hyena. Nobody is studying it; it is mostly viewed by local people as a problem animal."

As Tatjana and her team collect information on these species, they also build relationships with local communities.

"We have interactions with communities that live outside of protected areas. We learn of their challenges, and we are coming up with different possible ways that the conflict they experience can be mitigated," says Tatjana.

Snow leopards are harmless, but Persian leopards could harm people. Leopards will mainly kill livestock. Then people might retaliate.

"Despite all of your enthusiasm and best intentions, you still run into situations where you hear of putting traps out to kill the animal," she says.

For example, when a snow leopard kills livestock, it can have a terrible impact on a family.

"It could be a situation where suddenly all the food for your winter is gone, the sheep you were going to use for milk or meat is no longer there, how am I going to feed my family?" says Tatjana. "People will say, I will kill the snow leopard, sell what I can, then buy my sheep. Once you know that's the situation, you feel sorry for the snow leopard and the people."

Tatjana has unfortunately found dead leopards, which is why she is keen on removing traps.

"It is a stark reminder of the importance of our work, the effort that still needs to be put in, especially in areas where leopards are so low, when one individual matters," she says.

To protect the Persian leopard and other species, Tatiana relies on communication and education.

"The people that know there are leopards are the people that sometimes want to kill them, the poachers, the trappers," she says. "They are the most important people to engage in conservation, to understand *why* they are poaching. Sometimes it's basic food need, sometimes it's the love of being in the mountains. If we can change it to conservation, then some of the greatest protectors of leopards and their prey can be former hunters."

Her work with the leopards also helps local scientists.

"We support the local scientists in learning the tools of the trade, learning about camera traps, how to check them, how to do surveys of the important prey," she says. Tatjana works to ensure local staff get living wages and learn how to speak English. "Most literature and conversations about conservation happen in English, so it's an asset, to communicate, share, and be exposed to training opportunities."

A big part of Tatjana's work involves working with government officials. Persian leopards don't know about national borders. They roam where they want to. But government officials are concerned with national security.

"Border fences are being built, and some fences become impenetrable, for leopards, for prey," says Tatjana. "That has spurred an initiative and collaboration with Kazakhstan, but also with Iran. How border fences can be modified in a way that national security is not compromised but movement of animals is allowed."

Political Risks of Animal Research

Wildlife research scientists aren't immune from political conflicts. In 2018, several of Tatjana Rosen's colleagues associated with the Persian Wildlife Heritage Foundation (PWHF) were jailed in Iran and accused of spying.

It's a complicated situation, but Tatjana is concerned about the safety and health of her colleagues.

"The US NGO [nongovernmental organization] I used to be affiliated with supported (mostly through camera traps and technical advice) the work of PWHF," says Tatjana.

PWHF focused on conservation of wildlife in Iran, especially the Asiatic cheetah, which is critically endangered. Fewer than 50 Asiatic cheetahs remain in the world. All of them live in Iran.

"Iranian security services developed a case against PWHF because the founder of the US NGO supports a group called United Against Nuclear Iran (UANI). This then led the Iranian security services to believe PWHF was a cover for spies."

In November 2019, the detained Iranian conservationists were convicted of "contacts with the US enemy state" and sentenced to prison terms between four and 10 years. Appeals have failed so far to reverse the sentences.

Fortunately, Turkmenistan decided to join the Convention on the Conservation of Migratory Species (CMS). The convention includes a Central Asian Mammals Initiative, which creates an ongoing conversation between countries about addressing these threats to animals that can lead to practical solutions.

Tatjana was born and raised in Italy and the former Yugoslavia but sees her place in the world more broadly. She speaks seven languages. Her family is from the former Yugoslavia. They were born in the nations that are now Croatia, Bosnia, and Serbia. Her relatives are from a mix of Eastern European countries, stretching to Central Asia.

"My family did not talk much about their roots, they wanted to just be Western," she says. "Because of your accent or last name, if people think you are from the east or Central Asia, people think you are inferior, or less. I wanted to fit in, and for a long time I did not appreciate the complexity of my background. But probably the last 10 to 15 years, now I'm proud I have this complex background."

Rescue Mission Planet Earth

When Tatjana Rosen was a teenager, she joined a group of teens from around the world at a meeting in the countryside of the United Kingdom. Their job was to translate a United Nations document called Agenda 21 into a book that would appeal to young people. The book, called *Rescue Mission Planet Earth*, includes photographs, art, poetry, and more. It is still available today.

"The idea was to inspire young people with art, poetry, practical experiences, to care, to love nature and the earth," says Tatjana. "And to inspire their parents to change their practices and way of living."

Agenda 21 was meant to be a plan of action, developed from 1990 to 1992. The document talks about stopping logging, protecting oceans, and climate change. But it was written in very technical language and wasn't accessible to ordinary people. This experience showed Tatjana how important it is to make important information about protecting the environment as accessible to as many people as possible.

Her family's home region, the former Yugoslavia, experienced damaging civil wars from 1991 to 1999. Several republics declared independence, and the resulting wars left 140,000 people dead.

"I don't identify myself with one particular country, but definitely Central Asia and the Caucasus feel like home," she says. "What I think drove me back east to Central Asia was that combination of being interested in these incredible species, but also working in countries that have experienced the same things my family went through—loss, war, losing your home. Tajikistan was ravaged by a terrible civil war in the 1990s, the same time as the war in Yugoslavia. It's often been a conversation topic when doing our conservation work."

Growing up, Tatjana loved animals, especially dogs and horses.

Akhal-Teke Horses

When Tatjana Rosen isn't in the field in Turkmenistan, she loves spending time with Akhal-Teke horses. She also enjoys them at her home; she visits them on a friend's ranch in the Pacific Northwest of the United States. Akhal-Teke horses are considered one of the oldest horse breeds.

The signature coat of the Akhal-Teke is buckskin or golden. It is called *Bulanaya* in Russian. Buckskin

Akhal-Tekes seem to shimmer and shine.

Akhal-Teke horses are known for their incredible stamina. They are also intelligent and form strong bonds with their rider.

"My grandmothers lived in the countryside in Croatia, and I would spend a lot of time out in the forests, creating my own world," Tatjana says. "Some part of my family in Slovenia in the mountains had a nice amount of wildlife, and I had some very close encounters with bears. They did not scare me. I found them normal."

Tatjana thought she might be a veterinarian.

"But the war affected my family deeply," she says. "I wanted to be a peace negotiator working for the United Nations."

She followed this path and moved to the United States in 1998. She worked in a big law firm in New York City. Her love of nature continued, and she often did free work on cases resolving environmental disputes. Then two events made her rethink her life and priorities. Her law firm had been right across the street from the World Trade Center when the buildings were destroyed in the attacks of September 11, 2001.

"At first, I was going to transition and work for the UN on essentially resolving conflicts, but one person I deeply admired then was killed in an attack in Iraq in 2003," she says. "It brought to light some expectations about the UN that were not met. This incredible person who wanted to change the world was not supported in his work. He died."

That same year, Tatjana had a young daughter.

Facing so many challenges, Tatjana had a realization.

"Nature is where I find incredible comfort and peace," she said.

What she really wanted was to be a biologist. She went to night school at Columbia University so her infant daughter wouldn't miss her during the day. She continued her studies at Bard College, and then at Yale University.

"It was hard with a young child, but I managed," she says. "It was the program that made me realize what I wanted to focus on. In parallel I had started to volunteer on a grizzly bear project in Yellowstone that taught me how to be a field biologist. I learned camera trapping, collaring, looking for sign[s], and to identify the plants that were important for bears."

But Tatjana often struggled with the balance between fieldwork and being with her daughter. Tatjana's mother visited sometimes and cared for her daughter. Tatjana and her husband separated in 2009. The fieldwork and travel took a toll on their relationship. She faced difficult choices.

"I was told you cannot have it all. Employers said this is the life you choose, you cannot have both."

But she also worked for employers who recognized the importance of family.

"The truth is, everything is possible. The happier you are, the better you are at your job. When you become in charge of other people's lives, if you cannot ensure the person is happy in that sphere, it's going to affect the way they do their work."

Unfortunately, Tatjana has had very few female mentors in her career.

"I was lucky in my original bear fieldwork, I had an amazing female mentor in terms of her knowledge and encouragement, but she was pretty much the only one in 15 and 16 years," says Tatjana.

She still deals with the perception that because she is a woman she isn't strong enough. But there are glimmers of change.

"Central Asia is a very male-dominated society, but I receive the greatest amount of support from people in those countries," she says. "Once in Kyrgyzstan there was a minister in the government, and he praised me in front of everyone else. He said there should be more women in a position of leadership. I was shocked."

Even with all the challenges, she knows switching careers was the right thing to do.

"It's an incredible feeling to be out there. In the spring there is an incredible flower bloom, there are lots of almond trees, you smell the almonds," she says. "Then comes the summer, it gets very hot. You smell the burnt branches, and sand. Because it's close to the Caspian Sea, you are in an area that used to be part of [an] ancient ocean, you feel like you are on the beach.

All different smells, but they all bring this feeling of peace, and joy, freedom."

Tatjana uses social media often. She shares powerful photographs and words to highlight the contributions of local people.

"To remind the world it's not only us, there were a lot of conservation initiatives before we even came into the picture," she says. "Sometimes we have made things worse, we have disrupted the way people relate to nature."

She also enlists her daughter to help her connect with young people in the region. And she has received grants from National Geographic to bring stories of her research to classrooms in the United States.

"I tell young people to follow what makes their hearts tick," she says. "We tend to think in this box, only if you are a scientist you are allowed to talk about science and nature and conservation. My approach is that everyone who has a love for nature and conservation can do so much. Nature is an incredible space for healing. To protect it, there are so many ways."

Social Media

Twitter: @NarynTrosen

Instagram: NarynTrosen

Facebook: Naryn TR

Enikö Kubinyi:
Dogs, Wolf Pups, and Robots

Enikö Kubinyi knows old dogs can learn new things and that they can teach us a lot about people. Enikö is an ethologist, an animal behavior researcher, who works with dogs. She is the senior researcher at the department of ethology, Eötvös Loránd University, in Budapest, Hungary.

Enikö studies aging in dogs. In 2016, she received a Starting Grant from the European Research Council, considered one of the most prestigious grants in Europe. Winning this grant was a big deal because it usually goes to researchers in Western Europe.

"It was much bigger than any money I received in Hungary," she says. "I was able to establish my own research group."

The research group, called Senior Family Dog Project, has 12 scientists, including many at the beginning of their careers. They come from a mix of fields; some are psychologists, others veterinarians. They study three aspects of dogs and aging: genetics, neuroscience, and behavior. Behavior study is also known as ethology.

Enikö loves running her own lab, but it was a hard journey to get here. For many years, she debated whether to even keep researching.

"Before this grant, my salary was really low. I thought I would stop this and continue as, let's say, a bus driver because they make a lot more money, and I can give something to my children," she says. "The life of young researchers is not easy, at least not in Hungary."

Growing up in Budapest, Enikö loved animals and plants, but she couldn't have a dog.

"I lived in an apartment without a garden, and my parents did not allow us to keep dogs," she said. "I can understand why. But we had a lot of relatives in the country, [and] friends of mine also had dogs. Then when I was 16, I bought a dog with my own money. I bought a Hungarian vizsla."

Her parents had to let her keep the vizsla, whom she named Panka.

Enikö did well in school and continued studying biology and chemistry. Then, as a first-year student, she learned that Vilmos Csányi, a famous ethologist and the first in Hungary, was at her university.

"I had read all his books, and I contacted him, he was very nice. He invited me to work in his lab," she says. Vilmos studied the behavior of paradise fish, but right at this time he decided to switch to studying dogs.

"His colleagues were not really happy," she says. "They said the dog is not a natural species because they are domestic animals; therefore, ethologists cannot study dogs. They were primarily interested in the behavior of animals in their natural environment. But Professor Csányi realized that the natural environment of dogs is in their human family, so we have to study them there."

At this time there were no studies on family dogs, no literature, no protocols. And not long after Enikő joined the lab, Vilmos retired.

That's when she met her other mentor, Ádám Miklósi.

"He is currently the most famous ethologist in dog behavior and cognition. He has several hundred papers, lots of citations; on an international level he's very good," she says. Ádám developed the protocol of the experiments based on the study of primates and children and adopted methods of psychologists.

Enikő's work with Ádám was groundbreaking.

"One breakthrough was that in a series of experiments, we raised wolf puppies in 2001 to 2002, also dog puppies, and compared their behavior. We found a lot of differences," she says.

That research focused a lot on communication.

"Dogs focus on their owners. They are interested in the face of the owner, they are interested in what the owner is doing," says Enikö. "Wolves do not. They are much more independent and less vocal toward people."

The dogs were mixed breeds from shelters. The wolves came from a Hungarian man who worked with wild animals for filmmaking.

"When I worked with wolves, they loved raw food, full of blood. We used that to motivate them. Our 'wolf' clothes were bloody and muddy because wolf cubs jumped on us a lot," says Enikö.

One experiment they did was called pointing.

"Anyone can do this at home [with their pet dog]," says Enikö. "You take two flowerpots and put them down on the floor about two meters away from each other. Put a piece of food in only one pot."

One person holds the dog while another puts the pots on the ground a good distance in front of the dog. The researcher near the pots points to the pot where the food is.

"Dogs a few weeks old are very good at following this pointing, wolves are not," says Enikö. "Wolf cubs chose randomly. They do not care what is happening with people, they don't care if the human shows anything. Of course, they can learn it later on, but there is still the initial difference."

This difference between wolves and dogs makes sense to Enikö.

"Dogs depend on their owners. Their survival depends on their humans. Wolves depend on themselves."

Enikö and her husband recorded the work with wolves in a video called "Wolfwatching." They shared this film on YouTube on the research project's channel: The Family Dog Project.

Enikö also traveled to Paris, France, during her PhD studies in 2003. At this time, Sony unveiled a robotic dog called AIBO.

"We knew we had to investigate this robotic dog," Enikö said. Some of her first papers were about social learning. Social learning is when dogs learn behaviors from observing other dogs. She wanted to see if dogs would accept the AIBO as a real dog, and if they did, whether they would learn behaviors from AIBO.

"Adult dogs were not interested in the robot at all," says Enikö. "But some puppies attacked when the robot approached their food."

Enikö's French collaborator recorded her work with the robot dog and real dogs and shared it on YouTube.

It went viral and sparked collaborations.

"People in the UK spotted it. They also read the scientific article. They wanted to build social robots and realized our studies on dogs could help them," says Enikö. "Then we had a proposal together. We worked five and half years on a huge European project with the aim of developing social robots partly based on dog behavior."

These experiments led to the creation of an entirely new field of study: ethorobotics. Ethorobotics means creating robots with appropriate social and human behaviors. And Enikö was one of the first researchers in this field.

Enikö finished her PhD work and had twin daughters in 2004.

"You can imagine how tiring it was to have twins. I just tried to survive in the first two years and have some sleep," she said. "Still, I wanted to come back to the university, with the aim of studying personality in dogs."

She couldn't work as much while her children were young, but her husband and his parents helped a lot.

"Because of my family, I could basically go on with my research, not rapidly, but I did not lose contacts with my colleagues."

Her first grant proposal after having twins was successful. She had funding to study personality in dogs.

"We could hardly live on it, but at least I could do what I wanted to do," she says.

She continued to work in ethorobotics for many years. She had a third child, a boy, in 2011. She secured more funding whenever possible to continue her work.

Then a senior colleague, József Topál, advised her to apply for a grant supporting brain research, with the topic of brain aging in dogs.

"I knew nothing about this field, but I thought that using dogs as a model to study aging in humans was a really good idea," she says. However, the Hungarian funding body rejected her proposal.

So Enikö worked one more year on the proposal and sent it to the European Research Council.

"They were happy with the idea," says Enikö. They awarded her the five-year grant in 2016. Now, in her own lab, she explores the topic of aging dogs.

"Aging is a very important topic because human populations age globally, and it's a huge issue both economically and emotionally. In companion dogs, we can more easily study the biological background of aging than in humans," she says. "It is also important to study dog aging for its own sake. People value dogs so much, it affects them if they have problems."

Enikö's lab works with family dogs of any breed.

"We do not keep dogs in the laboratory. Owners come and visit us together with their dogs," she says.

The behavior tests are conducted in a big empty room on the sixth floor of a university building. The rooms smell like dog food and cleaning liquids. Researchers mop the room after each test whether or not a dog does its business indoors.

Owners bring their dogs for behavior tests. The tests last about 60 minutes with short breaks; after that, dogs lose focus. Researchers record the tests on video. They compare the behavior of young dogs to that of older dogs and examine how memory and cognition differ or change when they retest the dogs one year later. They look for specific genetic changes in older dogs.

"Dogs can develop dementia, we call it canine cognitive dysfunction, and it can be used as a model of human aging and dementia," she says.

In addition to tests and tissue analyses, dogs also get MRIs (magnetic resonance images). One of Enikö's colleagues, Márta Gácsi, was the first person to train dogs to lie motionless in an MRI machine.

"These dogs are able to lie motionless up to eight minutes," she says. "They do not move their head at all during the brain scanning. I think it's quite difficult, but Márta made them believe this is fun, and dogs love to please their owners and the trainers. They receive lots of praise and food for behaving well."

Another experiment uses electrodes to take an electroencephalogram (EEC) of dogs' brains. The test does not hurt. The electrodes are fixed on the skin with a mild glue, and the glue is washed off with warm water after the test. To do an EEC, it's better if the dogs are asleep so they don't move. So the dogs and owners go into the sleep lab.

"Dogs spend three and half hours in the sleeping lab with their owner. It's a very boring room with a soft mattress, so dogs quickly fall asleep and we measure their brain activity," she says. "Sometimes the owners fall asleep too."

The researchers are also studying the genomic sequence of very old dogs and comparing it to average-age dogs.

Enikö has worked with some of the oldest dogs in Hungary. One dog, Kedves, was 22 years old, and Buksi was 27 years old.

"Twenty-seven years old is really unique. I had the chance to meet this very nice dog and collect DNA," she says. "This is painless. We just rub the gums with a cotton swab."

They have found specific elements only in old dogs, but more studies are needed.

"The owner of Augie, a 20-year-old golden retriever who lives in the United States, sent me DNA by post," she says. "We are currently collecting DNA from dogs over the age of 20. If you know of some, contact me."

She uses social media to put out calls when they need volunteers.

"In Hungary, people mainly use Facebook, and I post in Hungarian," she says. "We also have an English Facebook page called Family Dog Project."

Enikö finds social media a valuable place to communicate about interesting research. She reviews scientific literature and shares it on both Facebook and Twitter.

"There are more than 50 people in our group studying dog behavior, but somehow I am the only person who is doing this on daily basis," she says. "I know a lot of researchers, and only a tiny minority is doing this on social media. I try to convince other people to join me."

Enikö also uses social media to discuss issues related to dogs.

"We have a lively dog ethology group on Facebook, there are more than 12,000 people. I share popular science articles there and sometimes collect data by surveys. When I asked what is the biggest problem in dog keeping, most people said there are too many. Shelters are overpopulated."

The First Animal Shelter in the United States

The Women's Animal Center in Philadelphia, Pennsylvania, is considered the first animal shelter in the United States. It was founded in 1869 by the Women's Society for the Prevention of Cruelty to Animals of Pennsylvania.

The founder, Caroline Earl White, along with 30 female activists, took over the pound. They changed it from a place where animals were caged and ignored and began helping lost and stray dogs find homes. They worked on other animal welfare projects, like installing water fountains for carriage horses around the city. They offered educational programs about how to care for animals.

The shelter they started still operates today.

According to Enikő's knowledge, there are 800 million dogs all over the world. And 80 percent are feral, or wild.

"They have a huge ecological impact. They make a lot of damage on local fauna," she says.

Land of the Strays

There is a legendary place for dogs in Costa Rica called Territorio de Zaguates, or Land of the Strays. Over 1,300 dogs live on 378 acres of land. The dogs are all rescues or strays and live full time at the no-kill shelter. People can come and visit the dogs, play with them, and adopt them.

It's more than a shelter. It's a sanctuary.

Founders Lya Battle and her husband Alvaro Saumet started saving dogs in their backyard in San Jose. They needed more space and in 2004, they opened the sanctuary.

The sanctuary is featured in the Netflix documentary *Dogs* from 2018.

While her focus is on domestic dogs, Enikö is interested in wild dogs too. She worked on a research paper with a person who lives in Bali. This research included volunteers completing personality surveys of wild dogs and adopted street dogs.

"It turned out the dogs seemed to have [a] happier life on the street than in the houses," she says. "They were less stressed, chased others less, less aggressive. I like this research very much. It was in contrast with the beliefs of Western people. We think when we give premium food and an expensive bed to our dog, they will be happy. But the life of a typical family dog is restricted, deprived, and usually quite unhappy."

Dogs at Risk of Extinction

When people think of endangered animals, dogs aren't on the list. But there are some dog breeds that could go extinct.

The nation of Bali in Indonesia has an indigenous type of dog called the Bali dog. Research and DNA samples show it is one of the oldest dog breeds in the world. It is unrecognized by kennel clubs. Until 2004, no other dog breeds could be imported into Bali. But when that law changed, new breeds arrived. Some bred with Bali dogs. The new dogs also introduced rabies to the island.

Now Bali dogs face serious threats that could lead to extinction. Many Bali dogs live on the streets, and local authorities often kill groups of the dogs because of concerns about rabies. Unfortunately, there are accusations that authorities are killing any street dogs without first checking if they have rabies.

In contrast, street dogs can decide whom they want to meet, when they want to pee, and where they want to go. They have more freedom. Enikö is well aware that dogs on the street might need veterinary care and can carry diseases like rabies and bite people. But she still has empathy for any captive animals.

"When domestication happened, it was not in the contract that 20,000 years later dogs will live in small flats, have to rest all day, and always be leashed outdoors," she says.

Throughout her studies, Enikö never had female mentors or professors. Enikö is a founding member of the Hungarian Youth Academy and member of the Young Academy of Europe. She helps female researchers, especially those with young kids, and does media communications. She is mentoring three PhD students now, and three have already defended their theses. She is also mentoring people who hope to submit proposals to the European Research Council.

Enikö loves her work, even if it isn't always easy.

"Finances is the biggest obstacle," she says. "Doing science is very interesting, but it's very hard living, and doing ethology is even more tough."

Social Media

Twitter: @KubinyiEniko

Facebook: Family Dog Project and Kutyaetológia

Instagram: @FamilyDogProject

Acknowledgments

Writing this book about wildlife scientists was a childhood dream come true. While we couldn't travel in 2020, each scientist transported me with their words to cool Appalachian forests, muggy Amazon jungles, and hot Australian gardens. We dove deep into the ocean and soared overhead the Antarctic ice shelf. We laughed a lot, and we cried. Their work is never easy, but it is always incredible. I am so grateful to all of the researchers who gave up their time and shared their stories with me.

Thanks to my agent, Miranda Paul, for her encouragement and support. Thanks to my editor, Kara Rota, for patiently answering all my questions.

Thank you to my fellow writers Jennifer Stephan, Carrie Koehler, Lisa Leinbaugh, Nicole McCandless, Kelly Conroy, Jessica Futtrell, Beth Skwarecki, and Briana McCormick. And thanks to the friends who suggested people to profile.

Thank you to my dog Beckham for his furry affection.

Finally, and most important, thanks to my family, Ed, Michael, Dylan, and Aidan, for believing in me—and for being quiet during the Zoom interviews.

Resources

Apps for Animal Allies

Merlin Bird ID will help you recognize birds by sight and song. You can then log the birds you see in eBird.

iNaturalist is a great way to snap photos and share them with the community. You can learn the names of insects, plants, fungi, and more.

Try Camera Trapping

If you have a backyard, you can buy a camera trap for under $100. Set it up in your backyard and record what animals pass through. If you can't get the camera, you can create a mud patch in your backyard and watch for tracks.

Look into Photo ID Projects

Help camera trappers identify animals on eMammal (https:// emammal.si.edu/participate) or Snapshot Safari (https://www .zooniverse.org/organizations/meredithspalmer/snapshot-safari).

Become a Citizen or Community Scientist

Some examples are FrogWatch (https://frogwatch.next
.fieldscope.org), The Great Backyard Bird Count (https://www
.birdcount.org), and Firefly Watch (https://www.massaudubon
.org/get-involved/community-science/firefly-watch).

Find more projects like these at https://www.citizenscience
.gov/catalog/#.

Take Action on Climate Change

Learn how to take action with organizations like Climate
Generation (https://www.climategen.org/take-action/act
-climate-change/take-action/) and EarthDay.org (https://www
.earthday.org/campaign/act-on-climate-change/).

Go Plastic-Free

Join the global movement working to reduce plastic pollution
on our planet. Learn more at https://www.plasticfreejuly.org.

Notes

Chapter 1: Corina Newsome

"The marsh has drawn blood": All quotes from original author interview with Corina Newsome on November 25, 2020, unless otherwise noted here.

Lucille Farrier Stickel directed the Patuxent: US Fish and Wildlife Service National Wildlife Refuge System, "Lucille Farrier Stickel: Research Pioneer," October 15, 2015, https://www.fws.gov/refuges/about /ConservationHeroes/stickelLucille_07232012.html.

By 2007, there were over: US Fish and Wildlife Service National Digital Library, "Lucille Stickel Oral History Transcript," October 27, 2016, https://digitalmedia.fws.gov/digital/collection/document/id/2142/.

Black Birders Week is a weeklong event highlighting: Jillian Mock, "'Black Birders Week' Promotes Diversity and Takes on Racism in the Outdoors," Audubon, June 1, 2020, https://www.audubon.org/news /black-birders-week-promotes-diversity-and-takes-racism-outdoors.

Chapter 2: Michelle LaRue

"The photos can tell us how many": All quotes from original author interview with Michelle LaRue on December 1, 2020, unless otherwise noted here.

For about two centuries, most stories: Cool Antarctica, "Antarctic History: A Time Line of the Exploration of Antarctica," accessed October 4, 2021, https://www.coolantarctica.com/Antarctica%20fact%20file

/History/exploration-history.php; Antarctic Online, "History: Introduction," accessed October 4, 2021, https://www.antarcticaonline
.com/history/history.htm.

"Hui Te Rangiora (also known as Ūi Te Rangiora) . . . is said": Priscilla
Wehi, "Following the Threads: A Short Scan of Māori Journeys to
Antarctica," *Journal of the Royal Society of New Zealand*, December
20, 2020, http://mc.manuscriptcentral.com/nzjr.

"that would violate the Antarctic Conservation Act": National Science
Foundation, "Antarctic Conservation Acts and Permits," accessed
October 4, 2021, https://www.nsf.gov/geo/opp/antarct/aca/aca.jsp.

In 2016, the Scientific Committee on Antarctic Research (SCAR): Amy
Mitchell-Whittington, "'Wikibomb' to Celebrate More Than 90 Antarctic Female Scientists," *Brisbane Times*, August 31, 2016, https://
www.brisbanetimes.com.au/national/queensland/wikibomb-to
-celebrate-more-than-90-antarctic-female-scientists-20160831
-gr5q3d.html; Scientific Committee on Antarctic Research, "Women
in Antarctic Research," accessed October 4, 2021, https://www.scar
.org/antarctic-women/; Wikipedia, "Timeline of Women in Antarctica," accessed October 4, 2021, https://en.wikipedia.org/wiki
/Timeline_of_women_in_Antarctica.

Who was the first woman in Antarctica?: Oceanwide Expeditions (blog),
"The First Women in Antarctica," accessed October 4, 2021, https://
oceanwide-expeditions.com/blog/the-first-woman-and-female
-scientists-in-antarctica; Christina L. Hulbe, Weili Wang, and Simon
Ommanney, "Women in Glacioligy, a Historical Perspective," *Journal
of Glaciology* 565, no. 200 (2010), https://www.igsoc.org/awards
/honorary/j10j211.pdf.

Chapter 3: Natalia Ocampo-Peñuela

"I actually collect bird scars": All quotes from original author interview

with Natalia Ocampo-Peñuela on December 21, 2020, unless otherwise noted here.

an article Elizabeth Kerr wrote: "A Woman Naturalist: A Personal Account of the Work and Adventures of a Woman Collector of the Wilderness of Tropical America," *Collier's*, July 13, 1912, 69.

A 2014 study revealed that about 1 billion birds: "Why Birds Hit Windows—And How You Can Help Prevent It," All About Birds, The Cornell Lab, May 5, 2017, https://www.allaboutbirds.org/news/why-birds-hit-windows-and-how-you-can-help-prevent-it/.

At Duke University in 2016: The Bird Collision Project—Duke University, "Window Film Magazine Story—Feb 2016," February 18, 2016, https://sites.duke.edu/birdcollisions/; Natalie Ocampo-Peñuela, R. Scott Winston, Charlene J. Wu, Erika Zambello, Thomas W. Wittig, and Nicolette L. Cagle, "Patterns of Bird-Window Collisions Inform Mitigation on a University Campus," PeerJ, February 1, 2016, https://peerj.com/articles/1652.

Chapter 4: Corrie Moreau

"It was like rotting flowers": All quotes from original author interview with Corrie Moreau on November 19, 2020, unless otherwise noted here.

"Army ants are top predators": John C. Cannon, "Pumas Engineer Their Environment, Providing Habitat for Other Species, *Mongabay*, December 17, 2018, https://news.mongabay.com/2018/12/pumas-engineer-their-environment-providing-habitat-for-other-species/.

They all leave the colony at dusk: Robert Taylor, "Australian Endangered Species: Dinosaur Ant," The Conversation, January 8, 2014, https://theconversation.com/australian-endangered-species-dinosaur-ant-21603.

An ant biologist holds a glass tube: Alex Wild, "Andy Suarez (University of

Illinois) and Corrie Moreau (Field Museum) use aspirators to collect ants from a leaf litter sample. Ant Course 2012, Uganda" (photo), Myrmecology—the Study of Ants, The Diversity of Insects (website), accessed October 14, 2021, https://www.alexanderwild.com/Ants /Myrmecology-the-Study-of-Ants/Personalities/i-hXQpTGM.

Generations of children who learned: Tanya Latty, "Hidden Women of History: Maria Sibylla Merian, 17th-Century Entomologist and Scientific Adventurer," The Conversation, February 20, 2019, https:// theconversation.com/hidden-women-of-history-maria-sibylla -merian-17th-century-entomologist-and-scientific-adventurer -112057.

Some people thought sunshine turned: Joyce Sidman, *The Girl Who Drew Butterflies: How Maria Merian's Art Changed Science* (Boston: Clarion Books, 2018).

She confirmed that insects: Maria Sibylla Merian, "An Eventful Life," accessed October 4, 2021, http://www.sibyllamerian.com/biography .html.

Chapter 5: The Bug Chicks

"Put up a picture": All quotes from original author interview with Kristie Reddick and Jessica Honaker on December 8, 2020, unless otherwise noted here.

They are called camel spiders: The Arachnid Order Solifuge, "Introduction: What Are Solifuges?" accessed October 4, 2021, http://www .solpugid.com/Introduction.htm.

They hunt at night and eat: James H. Thorp, "Arthropoda and Related Groups," Solifugae page, Science Direct, accessed October 14, 2021, https://www.sciencedirect.com/topics/agricultural-and-biologi- cal-sciences/solifugae.

People often think a solifuge is: Jessie Szalay, "Camel Spiders: Facts and

Myths," LiveScience, December 16, 2014, https://www.livescience
.com/40025-camel-spiders-facts.html.

While all arachnids have eight legs: The Bug Chicks, "Solifuge Arachnids
(That's Latin for Awesome)," accessed October 4, 2021, https://the
bugchicks.com/articles/education/solifuge-arachnids-camel-spiders.

Chapter 6: Lizzy Lowe

"Dead spiders were falling": All quotes from original author interview with
Lizzy Lowe on December 10, 2020, unless otherwise noted here.

"the variety of life on Earth": American Museum of Natural History, "What
Is Biodiversity?" accessed October 4, 2021, https://www.amnh.org
/research/center-for-biodiversity-conservation/what-is-biodiversity.

These two factors are called: Smithsonian Environmental Research Center,
"Biodiversity Assessment," accessed October 4, 2021, https://serc
.si.edu/research/research-topics/biodiversity-conservation
/biodiversity-assessment.

The number of species divided by: Science World, "Insect Biodiversity Survey," accessed October 4, 2021, https://www.scienceworld.ca
/resource/bug-diversity-hunt/.

"For example, a 4-by-4-meter": American Museum of Natural History,
"How to Calculate a Biodiversity Index," accessed October 4, 2021,
https://www.amnh.org/learn-teach/curriculum-collections
/biodiversity-counts/plant-ecology/how-to-calculate-a
-biodiversity-index.

"global crash in insect populations": Mark Rigby, "Insect Population
Decline Leaves Australian Scientists Searching for Solutions," ABC
Far North, February 23, 2018, https://www.abc.net.au/news/2018
-02-24/decline-in-insect-population-baffles-scientists/9481136.

Scientific American *reported large reductions*: Mary Hoff, "As Insect Populations Decline, Scientists Are Trying to Understand Why," *Scientific*

American, November 1, 2018, https://www.scientificamerican.com /article/as-insect-populations-decline-scientists-are-trying-to -understand-why/.

And in 2020, scientists published: Marlowe Hood, "'Warning to Humanity: Stop Killing Insects Now Before It's Too Late, Say Scientists," Science Alert, February 11, 2020, https://www.sciencealert.com/half-a -million-insect-species-face-extinction-and-we-re-doing-nothing -about-it.

"The International Union for the Conservation of Nature": Hood, "'Warning to Humanity.'"

But collecting is essential to entomology: Greg Pohl, "Why We Kill Bugs— The Case for Collecting Insects," *Newsletter of the Biological Survey of Canada (Terrestrial Arthropods)* 28, no. 1 (2009): 10–17, https:// www.researchgate.net/publication/228500262_Why_we_kill_bugs -the_case_for_collecting_insects.

Chapter 7: Jasmin Graham

"When we drag sharks up": All quotes from original author interview with Jasmin Graham on November 23, 2020, unless otherwise noted here.

"You have these pictures of scientists": "Don't Phone a Friend. Skype a Scientist!" Science Friday, July 7, 2017, https://www.sciencefriday.com /segments/dont-phone-a-friend-skype-a-scientist/.

"Our main goal is connecting as many people": Peter Haskell, "Have Coronavirus Questions? You Can Now Skype a Scientist," WCBS Newsradio 880, April 29, 2020, https://www.radio.com/wcbs880 /articles/news/skype-a-scientist-gets-you-answers-from-an-expert.

"A lot of times people might": Flatow, "Don't Phone aFriend."

In 2020, there were over 5,000: Haskell, "Have Coronavirus Questions?"

Eugenie Clark was a Japanese American: "Dr. Eugenie Clark (1922–2015)," National Ocean Service, accessed October 4, 2021, https://

oceanservice.noaa.gov/news/may15/eugenie-clark.html.

She learned to scuba dive and: Ashley Gallagher, "Eugenie Clark—The
Shark Lady," Smithsonian Ocean, March 2018, https://ocean.si.edu
/ocean-life/sharks-rays/eugenie-clark-shark-lady.

Eugenie proved it was possible: Brooke Morton, "Becoming the Shark Lady:
The Legacy of Eugenie Clark," Scuba Diving, September 2, 2015,
https://www.scubadiving.com/becoming-shark-lady-legacy
-eugenie-clark.

Chapter 8: Diva Amon

"Knowing what lives there": All quotes from original author interview with
Diva Amon on December 7, 2020, unless otherwise noted here.

The indigenous people are Carib and: "Trinidad and Tobago—History and
Heritage," *Smithsonian Magazine*, November 6, 2007, https://www
.smithsonianmag.com/travel/trinidad-and-tobago-history-and
-heritage-17893991/.

Modern Trinidad and Tobago: Bridget Brereton, "Trinidad and Tobago,"
Britannica, October 2021, https://www.britannica.com/place
/Trinidad-and-Tobago/People.

Dr. Sylvia Earle isn't a: "About Us," Mission Blue: Sylvia Earle Alliance,
accessed October 4, 2021, https://mission-blue.org/about/.

she's a water-breaking scientist: "Six Pioneers of Ocean Exploration Who
Happen to Be Women," Parley for the Oceans, accessed October 4,
2021, https://www.parley.tv/updates/2017/3/7/five-pioneers-of
-ocean-exploration-who-happen-to-be-women.

she launched Mission Blue through *"save and restore the blue heart"*: "About
Us," Mission Blue: Sylvia Earle Alliance, accessed October 4, 2021,
https://mission-blue.org/about/.

Projects like Solwara 1: Ben Doherty, "Collapse of PNG Deep-Sea Mining Venture Calls for Moratorium," *Guardian*, September 15, 2019,

Notes

https://www.theguardian.com/world/2019/sep/16/collapse-of-png
-deep-sea-mining-venture-sparks-calls-for-moratorium.

Chapter 9: Erin Ashe

"It lived in my consciousness": All quotes from original author interview
with Erin Ashe on January 29, 2021, unless otherwise noted here.

"boundary organization that bridges": "About Us," Oceans Initiative,
accessed October 4, 2021, https://oceansinitiative.org/about-us/.

Boat sounds make it hard: Oceans Initiative, "Secret to a Sound Ocean"
(video), accessed October 4, 2021, https://vimeo.com/77623625.

"whale watching can have an impact": BBC News, "Who, What, Why: Is
Whale Watching Harmful to Whales?", July 12, 2011, https://
www.bbc.com/news/magazine-14107381.

And as the Whale and Dolphin Conservancy points out: Whale and Dolphin Conservation, "Whale and Dolphin Watching," accessed October 4, 2021, https://us.whales.org/whales-dolphins/whale-watching/.

The Southern Resident killer whale population: Marine Mammal Commission, "Southern Resident Killer Whale," accessed October 4, 2021,
https://www.mmc.gov/priority-topics/species-of-concern
/southern-resident-killer-whale/.

In July 2018, Tahlequah gave birth: Lynda V. Mapes, "It's a Boy: Tahlequah's
Baby Orca Is Frolicking, Healthy," *Seattle Times*, September 23, 2020,
https://www.seattletimes.com/seattle-news/environment/its-a-boy
-tahlequahs-baby-is-frolicking-healthy/.

Jane is a marine ecologist: Home page, JaneLubchenco.com, http://gordon
.science.oregonstate.edu/lubchenco/jlcv.

"I believe that scientists have an obligation": Dilara Ally, "Science in Our
Society—Part 1. An Interview with Dr. Jane Lubchenco," *Molecular
Ecologist*, October 13, 2011, https://www.molecularecologist
.com/2011/10/13/science-in-our-society-part-i-an-interview-with

-dr-jane-lubchenco/.

During the COVID-19 lockdown of 2020, Erin: "Virtual Marine Biology
Camp," Oceans Initiative, accessed October 4, 2021, https://
oceansinitiative.org/virtual-marine-biology-camp-videos-more/.

Chapter 10: InvestEGGator

"I didn't want to just work": All quotes from original author interview with
Helen Pheasey and Kim Williams-Gullen on December 1, 2020, and
December 10, 2020, unless otherwise noted here.

Only olive ridley and Kemp's ridley: Outward Bound Costa Rica, "Sea Turtle Arribada in Costa Rica," December 28, 2015, https://www
.outwardboundcostarica.org/sea-turtle-arribada-costa-rica/.

"illegal wildlife trade is a": Jani Hall, "Exotic Pet Trade, Explained,"
National Geographic, February 20, 2019, https://www
.nationalgeographic.com/animals/reference/exotic-pet-trade/.

"Slow lorises are supposed to be protected": Jani Hall, "Are Humans Pushing
the Slow Loris to Extinction?" https://www.nationalgeographic.com
/magazine/2017/10/explore-animals-illegal-pet-trade-slow-loris/.

"There are ways to minimize risk": Latin American Sea Turtles, "Volunteer
Project in Pacuare," accessed October 4, 2021, http://
latinamericanseaturtles.com/volunteer-pacuare.php.

Only 1 in 1,000 turtles is estimated: Kaitlyn Bra, "Getting to Know the
St. Kitts Sustainable Destination Council: Dr. Kimberly Stuart," Sustainable Travel, November 27, 2017, https://sustainabletravel.org
/sdc-dr-kimberly-stewart/.

"forty percent of all plastic": PBS NewsHour, "Plastic Lasts More Than
a Lifetime, and That's the Problem" (video), September 25, 2018,
https://www.youtube.com/watch?v=khqzd1Lq1sI.

Notes

Chapter 11: Kirsten Hecht

"People say they have feelings": All quotes from original author interview with Kirsten Hecht on December 4, 2020, unless otherwise noted here.

In 2008, the International Union for Conservation of Nature (IUCN): Chris Mattison, *Frogs and Toads of the World* (Princeton, NJ: Princeton University Press, 2011).

Researchers are even more concerned about the lack: Cell Press, "Even More Amphibians Are Endangered Than We Thought," ScienceDaily, May 6, 2019, https://www.sciencedaily.com/releases/2019/05/190506124115 .htm.

Bertha Lutz was a herpetologist: Edith M. Lederer, "Researchers: Latin American Women Got Women into UN Charter," *AP News*, September 2, 2016, https://apnews.com/article/049889e630b748229887 b91c8f21e3d2.

She fought for women's right: Lady Science, "Feminism, Fascism, and Frogs: The Case of Bertha Lutz at the United Nations," 2017, https:// www.ladyscience.com/feminism-fascism-frogs/no32.

Chapter 12: Sneha Dharwadkhar

"At night the forest becomes alive": All quotes from original author interview with Sneha Dharwadkhar on December 17, 2020, unless otherwise noted here.

The Western Ghats are listed as one: UNESCO World Heritage List, "Western Ghats," accessed October 4, 2021, https://whc.unesco.org/en /list/1342/.

"Approximately 157 species of reptiles": Critical Ecosystem Partnership Fund, "Western Ghats and Sri Lanka—Species," accessed October 4, 2021, https://www.cepf.net/our-work/biodiversity-hotspots/western -ghats-and-sri-lanka/species.

"human–wildlife conflict": World Wildlife Fund, "A Biodiversity Hotspot,"
accessed October 4, 2021, https://wwf.panda.org/discover
/knowledge_hub/where_we_work/western_ghats/?.

"critical indicator of the health of the world's biodiversity": The IUCN Red
List of Threatened Species, "Background & History," accessed October 4, 2021, https://www.iucnredlist.org/about/background-history.

The Red List includes some success stories: The IUCN Red List of Threatened Species, "Grand Cayman Blue Iguana: Population," accessed
October 4, 2021, https://www.iucnredlist.org/species/44275
/2994409#population.

"there are more than 128,500 species": The IUCN Red List of Threatened
Species, "Background & History."

Chapter 13: Asia Murphy

"My goal was to get pictures": All quotes from original author interview
with Asia Murphy onNovember 17, 2020.

Chapter 14: Tatjana Rosen

"There was a Persian leopard paw print": All quotes from original author
interview with Tatjana Rosen on December 16, 2020, unless otherwise noted here.

"The US NGO [nongovernmental organization] I used to be affiliated with":
Murtaza Hussain, "Did an American Billonaire Philanthropist Play a
Role in the Imprisonment of Iranian Environmentalists?" The Inter-
cept, November 27, 2019, https://theintercept.com/2019/11/27
/iran-environmentalists-panthera-thomas-kaplan/.

PWHF focused on conservation: Kayleigh Long, "8 Conservationists
Convicted of Spying in Iran," EcoWatch, November 29, 2019, https://
www.ecowatch.com/iran-sentences-eight-conservationists
-convicted-of-spying-2641479414.html?rebelltitem=2#rebelltitem2.

In November 2019, the detained Iranian conservationists: Home page, Any
Hope for Nature (website), accessed October 4, 2021, https://
anyhopefornature.net.

Agenda 21 was meant to be a plan: United Nations Sustainable Development Goals Knowledge Platform, "Agenda 21," accessed October 4,
2021, https://sustainabledevelopment.un.org/outcomedocuments
/agenda21.

Akhal-Teke horses are considered: Equine World UK, "Akhal-Teke Horse,"
accessed October 4, 2021, https://equine-world.co.uk/info
/about-horses/horse-pony-breeds/akhal-teke-horse.

The signature coat of the Akhal-Teke: Akhal-Teke Association of American,
"Breed Colors" page, accessed October 18, 2021, https://akhal-teke
.org/the-breed/breed-colors/.

Chapter 15: Enikö Kubinyi

"It was much bigger than any money": All quotes from original author
interview with Enikö Kubinyi on January 22, 2021, unless otherwise
noted here.

The founder, Caroline Earl White: Christy Caplan, "The First US Animal
Shelter Was Founded by Women 150 Years Ago," Wide Open Pets,
accessed October 4, 2021, https://www.wideopenpets.com/first-us
-animal-shelter-founded-150-years-ago/.

They offered educational programs: Katie Park, "30 Philadelphia Women
Created 'America's First Animal Shelter.' At Last, They Get Their
Due," *Pittsburgh Post-Gazette*, April 10, 2019, https://www.post
-gazette.com/pets/pet-reports/2019/04/10/30-Philadelphia
-women-created-America-s-First-Animal-Shelter-At-last-they-get
-their-due-1/stories/201904100078.

called Territorio de Zaguates: Sarah Stacke, "Welcome to the Land of a
Thousand Stray Dogs," National Geographic, November 1, 2016,

https://www.nationalgeographic.com/photography/proof/2017/11
/land-of-strays/.

The nation of Bali in Indonesia has an indigenous: Bali Animal Welfare
Association, "Bali Heritage Dog," accessed October 18, 2021, https://
bawabali.com/resources/bali-heritage-dog/.

Unfortunately, there are accusations that authorities: Victoria Tunggono,
"Balinese Dogs Are Going Extinct if We Don't Do Anything About
It," Libero.id, January 2020, https://www.libero.id/detail/1048
/balinese-dogs-are-going-extinct-if-we-don-rsquo-t-do-anything
-about-it.html.